Amanda Jeffries

Straightforward

Advanced Workbook

MACMILLAN

Macmillan Education
4 Crinan Street
London N1 9XW
A division of Macmillan Publishers Limited
Companies and representatives throughout the world

ISBN 978-0-230-42348-0 Workbook
ISBN 978-0-230-42347-3 Workbook plus Answer Key
ISBN 978-0-230-42346-6 Workbook plus Answer Key and Workbook Audio CD
ISBN 978-0-230-42345-9 Workbook and Workbook Audio CD

This edition published 2013
First edition published 2008

This edition designed by eMC Design Limited
Original design by Oliver Design
Illustrated by Rowan Barnes-Murphy pp68, 88; Fred Blunt pp10, 37, 84; Annie Boberg pp16, 86; Chris Ede p9; Tim Kahane pp64, 66; Joanna Kerr pp5, 59; Julian Mosedale pp18, 67, 81
Cover design by eMC Design Limited
Cover photograph by Alamy/Images & Stories (main); Getty Images/Doug Chinnery; Alamy/Robert Harding Picture Library Ltd; Corbis/Roger Tidman; Corbis/Lois Ellen Frank; Corbis/Gerolf Kalt.
Picture research by Sally Cole

Authors' acknowledgements
The Author would like to thank Ruth Goodman, Lou Fonceca and Nicola Gardner for their hard work and helpful suggestions, and Yahia and Patrick for their support and ideas. Thanks also to Laila Meachin for her wonderful work on the design.

The publishers would like to thank all the teachers from around the world who provided invaluable comments, suggestions and feedback on the first edition.
The publishers would also like to thank the following people for their help and contribution to the second edition:
Tatiana Baytimerova (Russia), Lenka Boehmová (Czech Republic), Dr. Manuel Padilla Cruz (Spain), Svetlana Elchaninova (Russia), Jennifer Díaz Green (Dublin), Elena Mokeeva (Romania), Lynn Thomson (freelance editor), Amany Shawkey (Macmillan Egypt), Maria Teresa Rius Villaplana (Spain), Natalia Vorobyeva (Russia).

The author(s) and publishers are grateful for permission to reprint the following copyright material:
Page 90: Unadapted short story from Macmillan Literature Collections 'Twentieth-Century Stories', copyright © Mark Irvine and Ceri Jones 2011, reprinted by permission of Macmillan Education.
Page 21: John Carlin for an extract from "What sort of man makes millions from the poorest women in the world…" by John Carlin, *The Observer*, 05/11/2006. Reproduced by kind permission;
Page 33: Guardian News & Media Ltd for an extract from "Can she fix it?: Yes she can!" by Julie Bindel published in *The Guardian* 14/08/2006 copyright © Guardian News & Media Ltd 2006;
Page 39: Tribune Media Services for an extract from "Instant Expert: Stem Cells" by John Pickrell, published in *New Scientist Magazine* 04/09/2006 copyright © 2006 Reed Business Information – UK. All rights reserved. Distributed by Tribune Media Services;
Page 57: Extract from "Alternative tourist Trail: slumming it in Mumbai" by Justin Huggler copyright © The Independent 2006, first published in *The Independent* 25/07/2006, reprinted by permission of the publisher;
Page 9: Chris Calhoun Agency for the poem "On Turning Ten" by Billy Collins, copyright © Billy Collins;
Page 15: Dr Kerron Harvey for an extract from *Research Intelligence* (Issue 7) published in December 2000 by The University of Liverpool copyright © The University of Liverpool www.liv.ac.uk/researchintelligence;
Page 30: BHP Information Solutions Ltd for an extract from "Decide if running a business is for you" published on www.everywoman.co.uk copyright © BHP Information Solutions Ltd 2006;
Page 27: Nelson Mandela Foundation for an extract from the speech 'I am prepared to die', *Nelson Mandela's statement from the dock at the opening of the defence case in the Rivonia Trial* by Nelson Mandela, 20 April 1964, copyright © 2012 Nelson Mandela Centre of Memory. Reproduced by kind permission;
Page 27: Curtis Brown Group Ltd for a quote by Winston Churchill, copyright © Winston S. Churchill. Reproduced with permission of Curtis Brown Ltd, London on behalf of The Estate of Winston Churchill.

The authors and publishers would like to thank the following for permission to reproduce their photographs:
AFP p63(b); **Alamy**/P.Alvey p53(6), Alamy/Aurora Photos p56(br), Alamy/Dundee Photographics p69(cl), Alamy/ED Images p54(C), Alamy/T.Hill p15(tr), Alamy/Incamerastock p46(D), Alamy/A.Laming p53(4), Alamy/O.Maksymenko p46(A), Alamy/A.Nettle p13(cl), Alamy/A.Parker p53(2), Alamy/SJ Images p53(3), Alamy/Synthetic A. King p46(C), Alamy/Zefa RF p31(cr); **Brand X** p49(br); **Cartoon Stock**/E.Argo p34(cl), Cartoon Stock/N.Baker p17(bl), Cartoon Stock/N.Ford p22(bl), Cartoon Stock/S.Hutchinson p70(cr), Cartoon Stock/J.Morris p4(cl), Cartoon Stock/Naf p6(bl), Cartoon Stock/R.Thompson p41(br); **Comstock** p12(bl); **Corbis**/Bettmann p13(tl), Corbis/R.Chung p60(cl), Corbis/O.Fantuz p53(5), Corbis/L.Giraudou p15(cr), Corbis/Hero p78(tl), Corbis/M.Hunt/Huntstock p33(tr), Corbis/A.Ikeda/Image Source p54(A), Corbis/C.Liewig p21(tr), Corbis/ J.McDonald p46(E), Corbis/R.Olson p57(b), Corbis/C.Pertwee p13(bl), Corbis/P.Turnley p27(tr), Corbis/O.Wirtinger p80(cl); Corbis RF p15(bl); **Getty Images**/J.Sweeney p61(bl); **Getty RF** p42(bl); **Getty Images News** p27(br); **Getty Images Sport** p72(br); **Macmillan Publishers Ltd** p11; **Mary Evans**/Glasshouse Images p79(tl); **Pathfinder** p58(tl); **Rex Features**/Focus Images Ltd p87(tl), Rex Features/Moviestore Collection p51(tr), Rex Features/Newspix p45, Rex Features/Eye Ubiquitous p54(B); **Science Photo Library**/M.Agliolo p71(tr), Science Photo Library/3D4 Medical.com p39(b), Science Photo Library/NASA p75(br); **Superstock** p24(b), Superstock/Cusp p46(B), Superstock/Fancy Collection p28(tr), Superstock/Flirt p23(br), Superstock/Food Collection p46(F),Superstock/Somos p31(cl), Superstock/Travelshots p85(bl); **Stockbyte** pp53(1), 54(D); **Stone** p89(bl); **The Bridgeman Art Library**/Look and Learn p36(cr).

Printed and bound in Thailand

2017 2016 2015 2014
10 9 8 7 6 5 4 3 2

Contents

Writing

1A | All change

Change

1 Match the verbs in the box to their collocations 1–5.

adapt	convert	switch	transfer	vary

1 channels / seats / courses ________
2 money to a bank account / to a new team / to a new office ________
3 your diet / your routine / your intonation ________
4 to a new environment / to married life / to a different climate ________
5 dollars into euros / a house into two flats / to a different religion ________

'When you said you were transferring me to another office, I just presumed it would be one of ours.'

2 Complete the sentences with the nouns from the box.

adaptation	alteration	shift	transformation	variation

1 There has been a gradual __________ in people's attitudes to the environment over the last two decades or so.
2 I'd like to make a slight __________ to our original plan.
3 My son's academic performance has undergone a complete __________ since he transferred to the new school.
4 The film is a faithful __________ of Jane Austen's novel *Emma*.
5 The survey revealed widespread __________ in the cost of new houses across the country.

Vocabulary from the lesson

3 Choose the correct alternative, a, b or c, to complete the sentences.

1 We didn't have a serious conversation – just general ________ about this and that.
a) clatter b) chitchat c) chatterbox
2 The company did not want to become ________ in a costly legal dispute, and so the matter was settled out of court.
a) embroidered b) embellished c) embroiled
3 When she got her first salary cheque, she ________ it all away on clothes and expensive holidays.
a) fluttered b) flitted c) frittered
4 Music is a universal form of communication that ________ language.
a) transports b) transcends c) transposes
5 Even carefully-planned holidays can sometimes ________ awry.
a) get b) go c) give
6 When a couple first have a child, life can often ________ around the baby's needs.
a) revert b) revolve c) revolt

Dictation

4 **01** Write the text that you hear.

1B | First day

Simple & continuous verb forms

1 Complete the email with the verbs in brackets in the correct form.

File Edit View Favourites Tools Help Link

Hi Jess

How are you? I (1) ________ (*try*) to ring you all evening, but no reply. I wanted to say goodbye as I (2) ________ (*leave*) London tomorrow for a new life in Brazil! Yes, this is a major life change for me. But my job (3) ________ (*get*) more and more stressful recently, and I (4) ________ (*feel*) the need for a change of scene for some time now. Then, just before Christmas, I (5) ________ (*surf*) the internet when I (6) ________ (*come*) across an advertisement for a locum doctor in Brazil. So, to cut a long story short, I (7) ________ (*apply*) and they (8) ________ (*offer*) me the job.

It's hard to believe that this time tomorrow I (9) ________ (*sit*) on a plane on my way to another continent. I must admit I (10) ________ (*feel*) a little apprehensive right now, but I (11) ________ (*know*) it's the right thing to do.

Sorry not to be able to say goodbye properly, but if you get this email, give me a ring on my mobile — my plane (12) ________ (*leave*) at 4.00 tomorrow afternoon so you can catch me any time before that.

Lots of love

Emma

2 Find three sentences that are grammatically correct. Then correct the verb forms in the other sentences.

1 I see a friend tomorrow evening.
2 The weather is getting much warmer these days.
3 Don't phone me at 6.00 as I'll work.
4 I currently stay with friends while my kitchen is extended.
5 His son was often crying when he was a baby.
6 My boss is being rather uncooperative at the moment.
7 I've been driving 200km today.
8 My sister is always borrowing my clothes without asking.

3 Write sentences to describe the pictures, using the present perfect simple or continuous, with the words in brackets.

1 (it/snow)

____.

2 (he/build a snowman)

____.

3 (he/play in the mud)

____.

Approximation

4 Choose the correct alternative, a, b or c, that corresponds with the expression in italics (more than one may be possible).

1 There are *forty odd* restaurants in the town, so we won't have a problem getting a meal.
a) 40 b) 42 c) 43

2 It's *coming up to 8.00*.
a) 7.55 b) 8.00 c) 8.02

3 Let's set off at *five-ish*.
a) 4.30 b) 5.02 c) 5.45

4 It took *very nearly six months* to finish the extension.
a) seven months b) five and a half months
c) six months

5 It will cost something *in the region of €20,000* to convert the loft into a bedroom.
a) €18,000 b) €20,000 c) €40,000

5 Decide if the sentences are true (T) or false (F). Correct the false sentences.

1 The length of a marathon is 40 kilometres or so. _____
2 The record for running a marathon is just under two hours. _____
3 The world population is upwards of 6,000,000,000. _____
4 Something like 70% of the world's surface is water. _____
5 The height of Mount Everest is 12,000m or something like that. _____

1c | Growing up

Age

1 Match the words and phrases in the box to the sentences 1–6.

a middle-aged woman	a newborn
a senior citizen	a teenager
a toddler	a twentysomething

1 He often has tantrums, and his favourite word is 'no!' ______________

2 His voice has just broken. ______________

3 Her children have just left the nest. ______________

4 She's thinking of starting a family. ______________

5 He weighs 3.5 kilograms. ______________

6 She's drawing a pension. ______________

2 Complete the sentences 1–6 with the correct form of the verbs in the box.

come (x2)	get	have	side	turn

1 Her twelfth birthday was last month; she's just ______________ twelve.

2 He's eighteen; he's ______________ of age.

3 She's 42; she's on the wrong ______________ of 40.

4 He's fortysomething; he's ______________ a midlife crisis.

5 He's 63; he's just ______________ up to retirement.

6 She's 78; she's ______________ on for 80.

'For goodness sake, just pick one! I'm nearly seventeen!'

Reference

3 Complete the text with *this*, *these* or *those*.

In every culture, the journey between childhood and adulthood is punctuated by a series of minute and momentous transitions. (1) __________ vary from society to society, but in most cultures they might include having one's first boyfriend or girlfriend, leaving home, marriage, and having one's first child. For (2) __________ living in developed societies, such milestones as coming of age, obtaining a driving licence, voting, and entering and graduating from university are also seen as important, and many of (3) __________ events are marked by special celebrations. However, in some developing societies, (4) __________ period takes on a special significance, and ceremonies to mark major rites of passage are more elaborate than (5) __________ conducted in western societies. Some societies carry out lengthy and often arduous initiation ceremonies to mark the transition to adulthood of male members of the tribe. For example, (6) __________ boys who are crossing the threshold of puberty may have to be separated from their families and take part in arduous endurance tests. (7) __________ ceremonies also mark their eligibility for marriage, although (8) __________ will often also depend on how much wealth they acquire.

Substitution

4 Rewrite B's reply using appropriate substitution expressions.

1 **A:** How do your kids like their new school?
B: Joe doesn't like it, but Amy likes it.

______________________________.

2 **A:** Which shoes do you want to try on?
B: Those shoes in the window, please.

______________________________.

3 **A:** I don't think I'll be able to afford a mortgage.
B: I don't think I'll be able to afford a mortgage either.

______________________________.

4 **A:** How were your flights?
B: The flight from Heathrow was fine but the return flight was delayed by two hours.

______________________________.

5 **A:** My parents want me to settle down.
B: My parents want me to settle down too.

______________________________.

1D | The quarterlife crisis

Noun suffixes

1 Complete the text with the correct noun form of the words in brackets.

Following the (1) ___________ (*retire*) of the Head of Sales, and the (2) ___________ (*depart*) of the Assistant Head to our London branch, two vacancies have arisen in the Sales (3) ___________ (*Depart*). Applicants should possess (4) ___________ (*flexible*) and (5) ___________ (*enthusiastic*). (6) ___________ (*Patient*), (7) ___________ (*self-confident*) and the (8) ___________ (*able*) to make (9) ___________ (*decide*) are also an advantage. For details of the application (10) ___________ (*proceed*), please contact Mrs Doris Hancock.

2 Rearrange the upper case letters to make words that match the definitions 1–6.

A person who …

1 takes part in an event.
TRAPPINATIC ___________

2 cares for nature and the planet.
STENTINERVIMONAL ___________

3 writes a letter of recommendation for you.
EREEFER ___________

4 studies the past.
ONASHIRTI ___________

5 watches a sporting event.
TESCOTRAP ___________

6 takes part in a public protest.
NOSTRODRAMET ___________

3 Correct the wrong word in each group.

1 burial, occural, denial, survival ___________
2 maturity, generosity, certainty, fondity ___________
3 existence, absence, realizence, innocence ___________
4 obediency, pregnancy, urgency, accuracy ___________
5 investment, inhibitment, achievement, involvement ___________
6 awareness, tiredness, sincereness, seriousness ___________

Vocabulary from the lesson

4 Put the lines of the letter in the correct order.

Dear Angela

Can you help me? I feel I'm stuck at the moment, living at home and in a dead-end job. It feels like I'm just treading

☐ a at home from the harsh
☐ b down but without a good salary there's no way I'll be able to take out a
☐ c what it means to look after myself. I'd like to settle
☐ d mortgage on a house. What do you advise?
☐ e realities of life, and that I need to stand on my own two feet and really grasp
☐ f spice to my life. My parents tell me that I'm too cocooned
☐ g water and going nowhere fast. I'd like to get a more exciting and well-paid job to add a bit of

Translation

5 Translate the text into your language.

Gingerbread is the leading grassroots charity supporting and representing the interests of very nearly 2 million lone parents and their children throughout England and Wales. Founded in 1970 by a lone mother in London, it aims to help families to help themselves by supporting social networks of friendship and peer support, and providing help and advice to one-parent families. It offers a confidential free phone line, and organizes holidays and events for families on a low income. It also runs campaigns on various children's issues in partnership with other UK charities.

____

____

____

____

1 | Reading

1 Match the diseases in the box to the definitions 1–3.

chickenpox   measles   mumps

1 a disease that mainly affects children in which the neck becomes swollen and painful ______________
2 an infectious disease that most children get once, in which the skin is covered with red spots. It is a more serious disease in adults. ______________
3 an infectious disease common in children in which there are red spots all over the body and a high temperature ______________

2 Tick the diseases in exercise 1 you had as a child.

3 How do you expect a child to feel about becoming ten?

a) excited
b) sad
c) anxious
d) indifferent

4 Read the poem and choose the best alternative a–d for exercise 3.

5 Match the pictures A–E to the verses 1–5.

6 Match the words and phrases 1–6 to the defintions a–f.

1 sneakers	☐	a	starting to be ill
2 psyche	☐	b	emptied away like water
3 disfiguring	☐	c	number
4 digit	☐	d	sports shoes
5 drained	☐	e	mind
6 coming down with something	☐	f	spoiling the appearance

7 Choose the best answer, a, b or c.

1 Who is the 'I' in the poem?
a) a child who is approaching their tenth birthday
b) a child who has just become ten
c) an adult remembering their tenth birthday

2 Who is the 'you' in the poem?
a) an adult
b) a ten-year-old
c) an imaginary friend

3 Verse 1 How is the writer feeling?
a) physically unwell
b) upset at the thought of becoming ten
c) misunderstood

4 Verse 2 How does the writer remember childhood?
a) as a time of fun and enjoyment
b) as a time of uncertainty
c) as a time of imagination and a sense of power

5 Verse 3 What feeling is described in this verse?
a) uncertainty about what lies ahead
b) sadness that childhood pleasures no longer feel the same
c) worry about the responsibilities of adulthood

6 Verse 4 Why is this 'the beginning of sadness'?
a) it's time to stop playing and be realistic about life
b) adults do not enjoy themselves
c) all the writer's friends have disappeared

7 Verse 5 What feeling is described in this verse?
a) fear of the dangers of adulthood
b) awareness of the limits of one's own power
c) awareness of one's own vulnerability

8 What do you think? Choose the alternative, a, b or c, that matches your opinion.

1 a) I think the writer is a boy.
b) I think the writer is a girl.
c) I think it's unclear if the writer is a boy or a girl.

2 How did you find the poem?
a) depressing
b) poignant
c) uninteresting
d) thought-provoking

3 What is your own feeling about the end of childhood?
a) It is a difficult time for everyone.
b) It's an exciting turning point.
c) I've no recollection of a clear end to my childhood.

9 Which of the quotations do you think match the feelings described in the poem? Why?

1 "**It's never too late to have a happy childhood.**"
Tom Robbins

2 "**A simple child,
That lightly draws its breath,
And feels its life in every limb,
What should it know of death?**"
William Wordsworth

3 "**There is always one moment in childhood when the door opens and lets the future in.**"
Graham Greene

4 "**The older I grow the more earnestly I feel that the few joys of childhood are the best that life has to give.**"
Ellen Glasgow

Read & listen

10 **02** Listen to Reading 1 *On turning ten* on the CD and read the poem again.

A

ON TURNING 10

1 The whole idea of it makes me feel
like I'm coming down with something,
something worse than any stomach ache
or the headaches I get from reading in bad light –
a kind of measles of the spirit,
a mumps of the psyche,
a disfiguring chickenpox of the soul.

2 You tell me it is too early to be looking back,
but that is because you have forgotten
the perfect simplicity of being one
and the beautiful complexity introduced by two.
But I can lie on my bed and remember every digit.
At four I was an Arabian wizard.
I could make myself invisible
by drinking a glass of milk a certain way.
At seven I was a soldier, at nine a prince.

3 But now I am mostly at the window
watching the late afternoon light.
Back then it never fell so solemnly
against the side of my tree house,
and my bicycle never leaned against the garage
as it does today,
all the dark blue speed drained out of it.

4 This is the beginning of sadness, I say to myself,
as I walk through the universe in my sneakers.
It is time to say goodbye to my imaginary friends,
time to turn the first big number.

5 It seems only yesterday I used to believe
there was nothing under my skin but light.
If you cut me I could shine.
But now when I fall upon the sidewalks of life,
I skin my knees. I bleed.

B Collins

B

C

D

E

2A | Memory

Memory & memories

1 Complete the second sentence so that it means the same as the first.

1 I have memorized this poem and can recite it perfectly.
I know ____.

2 I can never remember what people are called.
I have a poor ___________________________________.

3 Whenever I hear this song, I remember my student days.
This song brings _________________________________.

4 I can remember every detail of my first day at school.
I have ____.

5 I feel sad and happy at the same time when I remember my first love.
I have ____.

Gerunds & infinitives

2 Read this letter from a headteacher to a parent, and insert *to* where it is missing in front of verbs.

Handsworth School

Dear Mr Marriott

I am writing with regard to Melissa's progress this term, which I regret say has been extremely disappointing. It appears she would sooner spend time going to town with her friends than attend classes, and her prolonged absences have made her fall behind with her coursework. Furthermore she seems have made no effort do her homework, even though she has been reminded on several occasions hand this in on time. In class, her apparent inability stop chatting has meant she has failed take in anything that has been going on. Making more effort listen to her teacher might enable her make some progress and help her improve her powers of concentration. As I am sure you will appreciate, we cannot let students get away with this kind of behaviour and she has been told in no uncertain terms that she had better change her ways radically.

Yours sincerely,

John Manwairing

John Manwairing

3 Delete the incorrect alternatives in these dialogues.

Receptionist: Would you mind (1) *take / taking / to take* a seat? The doctor will see you at five.

Patient: Yes, I would mind! I object to (2) *wait / waiting* over an hour to see the doctor! I'm used to (3) *be seen / being seen* immediately!

Alan: I've attempted (4) *get / getting / to get* my driving licence ten times now but I haven't managed (5) *pass / to pass / passing* the test. Is there any use (6) *have / to have / having* another try, do you think?

Sue: Have you considered (7) *have / to have / having* more lessons? And it might be a good idea (8) *change / to change / changing* your driving instructor. And I suggest (9) *stop / to stop / stopping* when the traffic lights are red next time, too.

Bridget: I hate (10) *come / coming* to these awful office parties. I can't stand (11) *make / to make / making* polite conversation and pretending (12) *enjoy / to enjoy / enjoying* myself.

Annie: Yes, I'm looking forward to (13) *go / going* home. I'd much sooner (14) *be / to be / being* in bed with a good book, and avoid (15) *have / to have / having* another late night.

4 Match the captions 1–4 to the pictures A–D.

A

C

B

D

☐ 1 He stopped to admire the view.
☐ 2 I remember combing my hair.
☐ 3 I remembered to comb my hair.
☐ 4 He stopped admiring the view.

2B | Memory man

Playing cards

1 Complete the text with the correct form of the words from the box (one is used twice).

bet	deal	deck	face	hand
object	shuffle	suit		

Poker is one of the most popular card games in the world. It is played by two to ten players, using a standard (1) ________ of 52 cards. The (2) ________ of the game is to win the biggest amount of money by guessing which player holds the best cards. This is calculated by means of different card combinations. Aces usually have a high value; the four different (3) ________ do not have relevance to the score. To play, the cards are first (4) ________ and then five cards are (5) ________ to each player, usually (6) ________ up, but sometimes (7) ________ down. Players then (8) ________ on which player has the best (9) ________ (ie the best collection of cards), by placing money in a 'pool' in the centre of the table. It is important that players do not reveal information about the cards they hold by not showing any signs of emotion – hence the expression 'a poker face'.

2 Complete the phrases to describe the cards.

1 The a____ of s____

2 The j____ of h____

3 The q____ of c____

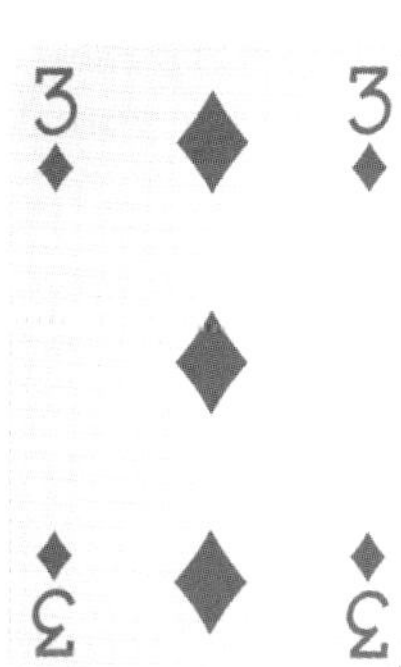

4 The t____ of d____

5 A j____

6 A p____ of c____

Vocabulary from the lesson

3 Rearrange the upper case letters to make words.

Success in the World Memory Championships involves (1) ____________ GREZIMOMIN large numbers of cards in the correct (2) ____________ CENEQUES, as well as numbers containing up to 2,000 (3) ____________ STIDIG. This is an amazing feat considering that normally only seven to nine are held in the (4) ____________ ROTHS-MERT memory. It can be achieved by a number of different techniques, including (5) ____________ TACIOOSSANI (making links between different items), location and journeys (ie the (6) ____________ LASPAIT facility of the brain), and imagination. Both (7) ____________ RESHEMESHIP of the brain are used to help (8) ____________ LACLER the information, including an important area called the (9) ____________ PUCOMPISHAP.

Dictation

4 **03** Write the text that you hear.

____

____

____

____

____

____

____

____

2c | Bicycle history

WAY

1 Complete the letter to a newspaper advice column with the expressions in the box.

a long way	in a bad way	ways	own way	way	in a roundabout way	out of my way	way around

Dear Angela,

For the last twelve months I have been sharing a flat with my best friend Charlene. We go back (1) _________ – to primary school in fact – and so I thought everything would work out OK. And at first it did. She was new to the area and didn't know her (2) _________, so I showed her the neighbourhood, introduced her to my friends, and so on. In fact, I went (3) _________ to help her settle in, and make her feel at home.

But then things started to change. She became more and more bossy, and if there was a disagreement she would insist on getting her (4) _________. I must admit that nine times out of ten I would give (5) _________ to her demands – anything for a quiet life. But now I'm fed up.

I've been trying for some time to tell her, (6) _________, to be more considerate, but she just doesn't seem to get the message. Now our friendship is really (7) _________ and I can see that if things don't improve soon we'll end up having a row. How can I persuade her to change her (8) _________?

VOCABULARY FROM THE LESSON

2 Label the picture with the words from the box.

chain	gears	pedal	spokes	tyre

3 Choose the correct alternative, a, b or c, to complete the sentences.

1 If you want to go to the beach, just ________ on your bike and you'll be there in five minutes.
a) skip b) hop c) creep

2 We are holding a meeting to try to ________ up support for the Cycling Proficiency training scheme.
a) drum b) tap c) beat

3 The penny farthing was the ________ of the modern bicycle.
a) precedent b) prerequisite c) precursor

4 The first bicycles did a great deal to ________ women from their restricted way of life.
a) eradicate b) emancipate c) elasticate

5 The injured bird started to ________ its wings, and finally managed to fly away.
a) flip b) flop c) flap

6 Cycling safety groups are planning to ________ for better facilities for cyclists.
a) lobby b) hobby c) tabby

TRANSLATION

4 Translate the text into your language.

Why cycle?

1 It's good for you

- *Regular cyclists enjoy a fitness level equal to that of a person ten years younger.*
- *Cycling at least 20 miles a week reduces the risk of heart disease to less than half that of non-cyclists who take no other exercise.*
- *During the rush hour, a bicycle is about twice as fast as a car – good if you hate traffic jams!*

2 It's good for your wallet

- *Bicycles require no road tax, no insurance, no licensing, no breakdown recovery services and above all no fuel bills.*

3 It's good for your world

- *Bicycles produce absolutely no pollution – they are a lot quieter too.*
- *Cars kill and injure thousands of people every year – bicycles don't.*

____

____

____

2D | A glimpse of the past

COMPARISONS

The Wright brothers made the world's first flight of 36.5 metres in Kitty Hawk in 1903. With a wingspan of 12.2 metres and designed for one person to fly, it weighed just 338kg, including the pilot.

The world's first supersonic passenger aircraft, Concorde, first took off in 1976. Designed to carry 100–150 passengers, it has a wingspan of 25.6 metres and a length of 61.66 metres. It holds the world record for circumnavigating the world in 31 hours, 37 minutes and 49 seconds. It was withdrawn from service in 2003.

Airbus 380, which made its maiden voyage in 2005, is the world's largest passenger aircraft, with a capacity of up to 853 passengers. It has a wingspan of 80 metres and is 73 metres in length.

1 Complete the sentences about the three aircraft above with the words and phrases in the box.

almost	by far	considerably	in common
little	marked	nowhere near	resemblance

1 The length of Concorde is ____________ the same as that of Airbus 380.

2 There is a ____________ difference between the passenger capacity of Airbus 380 and that of Concorde.

3 Kitty Hawk was ____________ as big as Airbus 380.

4 Kitty Hawk was ____________ slower than Concorde.

5 There is probably ____________ to choose between Airbus 380 and Concorde in terms of comfort.

6 The design of Kitty Hawk has little ____________ with that of Airbus 380.

7 Concorde bears a striking ____________ to a bird.

8 Kitty Hawk is ____________ the lightest of the three aircraft.

2 Change the underlined words to make the statements true.

1 Kitty Hawk carries the <u>most</u> passengers. ____________

2 The wingspan of Kitty Hawk is <u>slightly</u> shorter than that of Airbus 380. ____________

3 Concorde carries <u>more</u> passengers than Airbus 380. ____________

4 The wingspan of Airbus 380 is over <u>three times</u> as long as Kitty Hawk's first flight. ____________

3 Complete the second sentence so that it means the same as the first.

1 There is far more traffic on the roads nowadays than there was 100 years ago.
100 years ago there was nothing like ____________.

2 People had to work far harder then than they do nowadays.
Nowadays people don't ____________.

3 Men used to work in the mines, like their fathers.
Men used to work in the mines, as ____________.

4 A loaf of bread used to cost 1c, but now it costs $1.
Nowadays, a loaf costs a hundred times ____________.

5 People today are no happier than they were then.
People then were just ____________.

4 Rearrange the words in each line to complete the saying.

the know you study more more the you;
you more forget the you the know more;
less the more know you forget you the;
study why so?

____

____

____

____

2 | Reading

1 Use your dictionary to say whether the words in the box refer to pleasant smells (*P*), unpleasant smells (*U*) or neutral (*N*).

an aroma	a fragrance	an odour	a scent
a smell	a stench	a stink	a whiff

2 Which of these smells do you find pleasant (*P*), unpleasant (*U*) or neutral (*N*)?

boot polish _____
mustard _____
cloves _____
newly open drains _____
cut grass _____
petrol _____
freshly-baked bread _____
seaweed _____
fried onions _____
sweaty socks _____
ink _____

3 Read the statements and say whether you think they are true (T) or false (F).

1 The sense of smell triggers more memories of the past than the other four senses (sight, sound, taste and touch). _____
2 Memories retrieved by the sense of smell have a high emotional content. _____
3 Animals have a more developed sense of smell than humans. _____
4 People vary greatly in their response to smells. _____
5 The author Marcel Proust found that smells helped him to write. _____
6 The sense of smell is probably linked to a relatively primitive and unconscious region of the brain. _____
7 The sense of smell could be used to help some victims of memory loss. _____

4 Read the article and say whether it provides any scientific evidence to support any of the statements in exercise 3.

5 Read the article again and choose the best title a–e for the paragraphs 1–5.

☐ a Interpreting the results
☐ b Experimental research
☐ c The five senses
☐ d A personal example
☐ e Striking results

6 Match the definitions 1–10 to the words and phrases highlighted in the article.

1 based on someone's personal experience or information rather than on facts that can be checked _____
2 a range of measurements in a particular system _____
3 based on real experience or scientific experiments, rather than on theory _____
4 to discover, prove or decide that something is true _____
5 information that you discover, or opinions that you form after doing research _____
6 a particular period of time during the development of something _____
7 a research project that examines a problem or a particular subject _____
8 a person or animal that is used in a medical or scientific test _____
9 when two things, such as statements or calculation, match each other _____
10 to consider that someone or something has a particular quality or has achieved a particular standard _____

7 Complete the summary of Dr Chu's research with the words from exercise 6 in their correct form.

There is a good deal of (1) _______________ evidence that the sense of smell can trigger vivid and detailed memories of people's childhood, which also (2) _______________ Dr Chu's own personal experience. However, little (3) _______________ research has been carried out in this area. So he designed a major (4) _______________ to (5) _______________ whether memories triggered by smell differed from those triggered by words or images. The investigation consisted of two (6) _______________. In the first, all (7) _______________ had to give details of memories retrieved by verbal prompts. In the second, four groups were exposed to different stimuli, and had to (8) _______________ how they felt on a standard (9) _______________. Chu's striking (10) _______________ showed that memories retrieved by related smells were more vivid and focused than those triggered by any of the other stimuli. This has led him to formulate the hypothesis that the sense of smell is linked to a more primitive area of the brain.

READ & LISTEN

8 **04** Listen to Reading 2 *Sniffing back the years* on the CD and read the article again.

SNIFFING
BACK THE YEARS

1

The renowned author Marcel Proust suffered from 'writer's block' – surprisingly, perhaps, given his prodigious output. He overcame one major episode thanks to the aroma of tea and cakes, which triggered a flood of memories – and new material for his novel. It's not unusual to find a smell from the past triggering a memory, as Dr Simon Chu knows from personal experience. 'I spent part of my childhood in a village in Hong Kong's new territories,' he explains, 'and the whiff of open drains takes me straight back there, to one particular incident when I was attacked by a giant bee.'

2

His experience tallied with anecdotal evidence suggesting that memories retrieved by smells are very vivid and very detailed, that the remembered events happened early in life and that they were very emotional. However, there has been very little empirical research in this area, despite the fact that our perception of the world is developed in large part from information conveyed by sight, hearing, touch, taste – and smell.
'Some people believe that humans have less finely-tuned olfactory equipment than many other species', says Simon Chu, a member of the University of Liverpool's Psychology Department. 'But people working in the wine and perfume businesses learn to discriminate between different aromas and derive information from them, which suggests that's not necessarily the case.'

3

Dr Chu has chosen to explore this area using experimentation. In a major study on odour and autobiographical memory, he carried out a series of phased experiments designed to establish whether memories triggered by smell differed significantly from those triggered by words or images. In the first phase of the experiment, all the subjects listened to a series of words, and details of any memories associated with particular words were tape-recorded. In the second phase, the subjects were divided into four different groups and were asked to respond to either words, images, random smells or related smells.

In both phases, whenever a memory was retrieved, the subjects were asked to rate how emotional they felt, using a standard scale. The smells ranged from cheese, oranges, cloves, curry, mustard, vinegar, wine and coffee to ink, boot polish and petrol – chosen because they haven't changed significantly over time and they were likely to be familiar, culturally.

4

It turns out that smell is a very individual phenomenon, and only 40% of these smells actually triggered memories, compared to 95% of the words read by the subjects. However, the memories retrieved by related smells contained far greater details than those retrieved by the original word – whereas random smells and pictures did not have this effect. 'These particular memories were very focussed', Simon comments. 'For instance, the smell of boot polish reminded one subject of an unexpected visit from a long-lost relative. For another subject, the smell of fruit brought back memories of falling out of a tree. The memories retrieved by smell were also far more emotional than most autobiographical memories. The difference was very striking.'

5

So few people are researching this area, there isn't yet a well-developed framework for interpreting this finding. Though the part of the brain which processes smells is closely linked to regions which are responsible for memory, Simon Chu thinks that memories retrieved by smell may be stored or retrieved differently. One day, smell's potency as a retrieval device might even help treat cases of amnesia where all other methods of retrieving information fail – though it is unlikely to impact on amnesia caused by organic brain damage.

3A | Enough is enough

Adding emphasis with auxiliary verbs

1 Match the speech bubbles 1–5 to the pictures A–E.

1 *Do come in.*

2 *Do forgive the mess.*

3 *Do help yourself to more cake.*

4 *Do take a seat.*

5 *Sorry I interrupted you - do go on.*

2 Write a response to the comment using an appropriate form of the verb underlined, an emphatic adverb (*really*, *certainly* or *definitely*) and auxiliary *do*, *does* or *did*.

How well the football team played!
Yes, they certainly did play well, didn't they?

1 John seems to like his new job now.

______________________________________.

2 How beautiful those flowers smell!

______________________________________.

3 How strange it felt to say goodbye!

______________________________________.

4 What an excellent chef your brother is!

______________________________________.

5 I worked very hard to pass the exam.

______________________________________.

6 You need to do more practice of this.

______________________________________.

(Not) having enough

3 Match the sentence beginnings 1–8 in column A to the endings a–h in column B.

A

1 Unfortunately my salary is not enough to meet
2 We are well off
3 The current transport system is perfectly
4 During a war, fresh fruit and vegetables are often
5 The hotel is modern and clean, but sadly lacking
6 During the recent drought, water
7 Can you give me a hand? I'm a bit short
8 There are plenty

B

☐ a in atmosphere.
☐ b of employment opportunities in the company.
☐ c adequate for most people in my town.
☐ d in short supply.
☐ e the needs of my family.
☐ f for hospitals in my town.
☐ g shortages caused problems for many households.
☐ h of time today.

Dictation

4 **05** Write the text that you hear.

____

____

____

3B | Rubbish!

Rubbish

1 Complete the crossword. Find the mystery word.

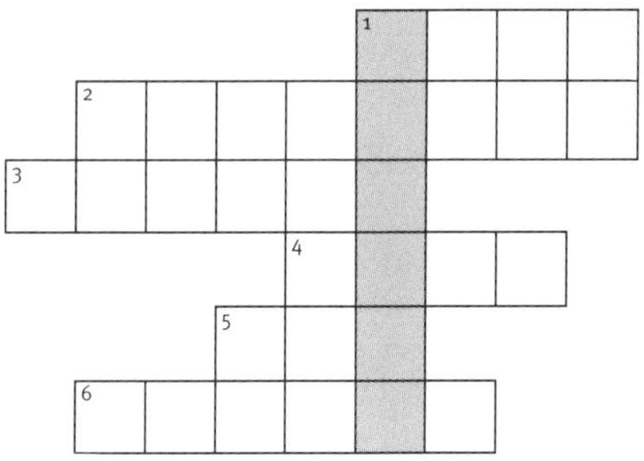

1 A large metal container in which you can throw away bulky items.
2 The vehicle used by dustmen to take away household rubbish.
3 Rubbish that people drop in public places.
4 You can put glass in a bottle _______ to be recycled.
5 The site where a town's rubbish is taken.
6 A general word for *rubbish*.

2 Complete the sentences 1–6 in column A with the phrases a–f in column B.

A
1 His house is always such a tip,
2 The town I live in is an absolute dump;
3 I'm not a great fan of junk food,
4 He always talks a load of rubbish,
5 The critics trashed the film,
6 He was thrown out of school;

B
☐ a it's so dirty, and there's absolutely nothing to do at night.
☐ b you can't believe a word he says.
☐ c I prefer something healthier.
☐ d I don't know why he can't tidy it up.
☐ e he was always skipping classes.
☐ f but I really enjoyed it.

'... And I only went inside for a minute ...'

Fronting

3 Complete the letter to the newspaper with the expressions a–g.

Dear Sirs,

I am writing to complain about the recent outbreak of graffiti-writing in our town centre.
I was shocked when I recently went with a friend to visit the new Royal Arts Centre in Westbrook Park. (1) _____ political slogans, obscene messages and the most disgusting pictures. (2) _____ the bus shelters, where, in addition to the graffiti, windows had been smashed and seats vandalized. I cannot understand why no one seems bothered about this antisocial behaviour. (3) _____ the fact that the police seem to turn a blind eye to what is going on. What is the point of having laws to protect our environment if they are never enforced? (4) _____, I have even heard people praising this public eyesore as 'urban art'.
(5) _____ I am at a loss to understand. (6) _____ to encourage artistic talent in our young people, surely there are better ways to practise than by defacing the walls of our public buildings? I have already written to the council to complain about this; (7) _____ it remains to be seen.

Yours faithfully,

Agnes Blenkinsop

a Strange as it may seem
b Particularly annoying is
c Sprayed all over the walls were
d Important though it is
e Quite what the attraction is
f whether or not they will take action
g Even worse were

3c | Competitive eating

Excess

1 Complete the captions 1–5 with the words in the box, then match them to the pictures A–E.

in all things	in excess of	over the top
to excess	to extremes	

1 After intensive training, Basil was able to reach speeds _______________ 1kph.
2 Tania started to wonder if she was taking fitness _______________.
3 Dennis went _______________ to make Ruby feel welcome.
4 Gregory's motto was moderation _______________.
5 Shopping _______________ was Daisy's weakness.

A

B

C
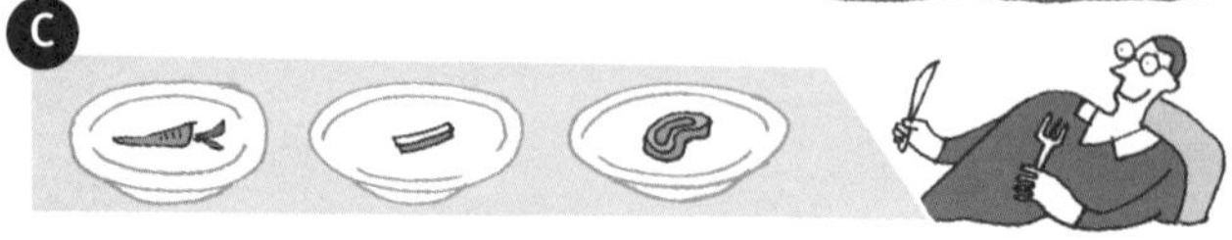

D

E

2 Complete the sentences with an adjective with the prefix *over-*.

1 With the childcare and household chores on top of a full-time job, Amelia is very _______________.
2 You need to be very careful with what you say to Jenny – she's rather _______________ and gets upset very easily.
3 The film received fantastic reviews, but personally I felt it was _______________.
4 We had to pay 20 euros for two coffees, which I thought was terribly _______________.
5 You'd better take a nap now – if you get _______________ you won't work as well.

Vocabulary from the lesson

3 Choose the correct alternatives to complete the text.

Arnold was so hungry that he (1) *grabbed / crabbed / drabbed* a packet of biscuits from the shelf and (2) *foxed / wolfed / pigged* the whole packet down in two minutes flat, nearly (3) *chucking / cheeking / choking* as he did so. Then he devoured a bowl of ice cream, (4) *licking / slicking / flicking* the bowl clean when he had finished. Finally he tucked into a huge steak, (5) *mitigating / manipulating / masticating* each mouthful carefully – 'I try to avoid getting indigestion if I can possibly help it', he (6) *congested / confided / configured*.

Translation

4 Translate the text into your language.

A new illness is sweeping the nation: 'affluenza'. Derived from the word 'affluence', or wealth, it is a psychological illness affecting people who have too much money, characterized by feelings of depression, guilt and lack of motivation. It is the product of our modern materialistic, competitive and individualistic society, and symptoms include overconsumption, compulsive shopping, high debt, overwork, wastefulness and stress.

So what is the treatment for affluenza? Psychologists say that what we need to do is adopt a simpler and less possession-driven lifestyle, and reduce our spending habits. We should save more money, stick to a realistic budget, and avoid impulse buys and using a credit card unless we have the cash to pay it off. Above all, we should make time for family and friends, and what we consider important in life, rather than the mindless pursuit of success and material wealth.

3D | A cautionary tale

Cleft sentences

EXCESS BAGGAGE

Most people either avoid travelling with excess baggage, or arrange for it to be transported later. But the millionaire television producer Darren Blackwell found a novel solution to the problem. When the pilot of his private jet told him that there was no room to carry all of his luggage, he decided to rent another for $20,000 to take it from Los Angeles to the Bahamas. Darren and his wife Linda had been on holiday in the Caribbean where he threw a huge party last week in Aruba for his birthday, which was attended by several celebrities. While he was there, Darren also paid to fly a chef in from nearby St Vincent because Linda was not satisfied with the one they had during their holiday.

1 Underline the wrong information about the article in these sentences. Then correct them, using a cleft structure with *it was*, as in the example:

Darren paid $200 to transport his excess baggage.
No, it was $20,000 dollars that he paid.

1 His wife told him there was no room for his luggage.

_______________________________________.

2 He hired a helicopter to carry his excess baggage.

_______________________________________.

3 He threw a huge party in St Vincent.

_______________________________________.

4 He threw a party because he was getting married.

_______________________________________.

5 He paid to fly a personal trainer in from St Vincent.

_______________________________________.

6 Darren was not pleased with the chef they had during their holiday.

_______________________________________.

2 Rewrite the sentences, using a *what* clause, to stress the underlined part of the sentence.

Examples:
John loves sport. (*object*)
What John loves is sport.
John goes for a jog every morning. (*verb*)
What John does every morning is go for a jog.
John won the race. (*verb*)
What happened was that John won the race.

1 He broke his ankle.

_______________________________________.

2 He broke the record.

_______________________________________.

3 It started to rain.

_______________________________________.

4 He's overworking.

_______________________________________.

5 He needs a rest.

_______________________________________.

6 He shouldn't work so hard.

_______________________________________.

Adjective affixes

3 Complete the table with the words in the box in the correct form.

advantageous advisable careful cooperative
courteous decisive deserving informative
powerful receptive respectful substantial

UN-	*DIS-*
-LESS	*IN-*

4 Use the positive or negative form of the adjectives from exercise 3 to replace the phrases in italics in the text.

Do you have neighbours from hell?
Do you feel *that you can't do anything* (1) ____________ to deal with noisy neighbours who insist on playing music at full volume, banging doors and shouting at the top of their voices? Every year, local government officers receive a *large* (2) ____________ number of complaints about excessive noise from neighbours. Many councils provide leaflets that are very *full of helpful facts* (3) ____________, telling you what you should do in this situation. The most important thing is to be *sure about what you are doing* (4) ____________ but *courteous* (5) ____________ when approaching your neighbour. Often people are unaware that they are causing a problem; most will be *willing to listen* (6) ____________ to your complaints, and only too glad to do what they can to reduce noise. However, if your neighbours are *unwilling to do what you request* (7) ____________, it is *a good idea* (8) ____________ to keep a diary recording dates, times and cause of the noise. However, try to resolve problems in a friendly way.

3 | Reading

1 Use your dictionary to match the adjectives 1–5 to the nouns a–e.

1	abject	☐ a	crank
2	exorbitant	☐ b	resources
3	innovative	☐ c	interest rates
4	scarce	☐ d	poverty
5	well-meaning	☐ e	system

2 Read the article. How does the writer describe Mohammad Yunus?

1 An impossible dreamer
2 A hard-headed businessman
3 A visionary philanthropist
4 A successful billionaire

3 Read the article again. Choose the best alternative, a or b, to complete the sentences.

1 Yunus developed Grameen
a) to improve the lives of the poor.
b) as a way of making money.

2 The rural workers Yunus met were trapped in poverty because
a) they could not afford to take out loans.
b) they had to pay back the loan sharks.

3 Grameen is revolutionary because
a) it lends money to poor people.
b) it does not demand evidence that loans can be repaid.

4 Grameen differs from other banks in that
a) it does not charge interest rates.
b) it charges low interest rates.

5 The women do not default on their loans from Grameen because
a) they would not have other chances to borrow from Grameen.
b) they are hardworking and motivated.

6 Grameen
a) does not make a profit.
b) uses its profits to develop the business.

7 Yunus believes loans are better than handouts because
a) they encourage people to develop skills.
b) he does not support welfare schemes.

4 Match the highlighted words and phrases in the article to the definitions 1–7.

1 a difficult or unpleasant situation that is not easy to get out of ______________
2 an amount of money or goods given to people who need them ______________
3 existing, happening or spreading in an uncontrolled way ______________
4 fail to pay money that you owe ______________
5 property that you agree to give to a bank if you fail to pay back money that you have borrowed ______________
6 someone who lends money to people and charges them a very high rate of interest ______________
7 with no money or possessions ______________

5 Read the article again and underline five examples of cleft sentence structures.

6 What do you think? Which is the best way to help people in developing countries? Choose the phrase, 1, 2, 3, or 4, which best matches your opinion and say why.

1 Give financial aid to the most destitute
2 Improve the education system
3 Develop the overall national economy
4 Provide loans for small businesses

READ & LISTEN

7 **06** Listen to Reading 3 *Banker to the poor* on the CD and read the article again.

BANKER TO THE POOR

John Carlin meets the 'World's Banker to the Poor', Mohammad Yunus, in Bangladesh.

If a man begins a speech preaching the 'firm, deep, passionate' belief that 'we can create a world free of poverty', you might find yourself admiring the sentiment, but struggle to shake off the suspicion that he is a well-meaning crank. Until, that is, you discover that he happens to be a professor of economics, a Nobel Peace Prize recipient and one of the most successful capitalists alive; a businessman who started a bank with a staff of two that today employs 20,000 people and has spawned eighteen other companies, one of them the biggest mobile-phone network in South Asia. And all the more so as the particular brand of capitalism to which he has dedicated his life sees not profit-making, but helping the wretched of the earth, as its primary mission.

Seen by many as a visionary genius, Muhammad Yunus is to poverty as Bill Gates is to computer software. Only that Yunus's business exponentially flourishes in his native Bangladesh, a country with a population of 145 million, most of whom live in abject poverty, and where illiteracy is rampant. And it is the poorest among the poor in this country whom Yunus has selected as the focus for his experiment: its women.

It was while on a field trip to a destitute rural community in southern Bangladesh that Yunus conceived his revolutionary idea. Interviewing a local woman who made bamboo stools, he learned that, lacking any savings or capital, she had to borrow the equivalent of 15p to buy bamboo for each stool. But after she had repaid the exorbitant interest rates demanded by the loan sharks, she only made 1p profit on each stool. Yunus found 41 other workers in a similar predicament and lent them the cash in his pocket as an experiment to help them break out of the vicious circle of poverty. His trust was rewarded; they paid him back and their businesses flourished.

Yunus went on to develop his innovative system of 'microcredits', ie making small loans available to needy entrepreneurs at affordable interest rates. What was original and utterly subversive about his plan was that he decided to lend lots of small amounts to the poor with no collateral, and on the basis of trust, not legal contracts. Within six years he had persuaded the institutional banks to lend him the money he needed and also to offer 50–50 parity between the sexes. What he found was that not only were the women repaying the money more reliably than the men, but that the small amounts of money going through the women brought much more benefit to the family, as it was they who had trained themselves to manage scarce resources, and were thus able to bring that efficiency to bear on the loans.

Yunus formally founded Grameen – which means 'village' in Bengali – as a bank in 1983 and, ever since, it has lent money to individuals, 97 per cent of whom are women, and all of whom are below the poverty line. Loans are often very small – as little as £20 – and recipients work in small groups, on the strict understanding that should one member of the group default, the others will be liable to repay their debt. The bank demands repayments very quickly, but in tiny instalments. Borrowers are typically hardworking, motivated, reliable and themselves altruistic, often creating collective, grass roots enterprises that benefit the whole community. Yunus has found that they will cling tenaciously to the one chance the bank offers them, fully aware that defaulters can never apply for another loan.

Today, Grameen operates in 70,000 villages, and has 2,200 branches and 6.6 million borrowers. To the bafflement of commercial bankers its microcredit system works, as Yunus likes to say, 'like clockwork'. The loan-default rate, the envy of any mainstream bank, is less than 1.5 per cent. Grameen has consistently reported annual profits most years, all of which are ploughed back into the scheme, which never stops growing. The model of microcredits has been imitated in more than 80 countries, reaching 100 million people worldwide.

Yunus, whilst not opposing welfare schemes per se, rejects charity as a long-term strategy for addressing the global imbalances between rich and poor. What he believes is that people are better off with a loan than with a handout: 'Give a man a fish, and you feed him for a day,' the old adage runs: 'Teach him to fish, and you feed him for a lifetime.'

4A | Voicing complaints

Ways of speaking

1 Delete the incorrect alternatives.

1 I can't stand the way she's always *moaning* / *whispering* / *stuttering*; I wish she'd be more positive.
2 I wish you would speak more clearly – it's hard to understand you when you *bellow* / *moan* / *mutter* like that.
3 You should see a speech therapist to see if she can help you stop *snapping* / *stuttering* / *shrieking*.
4 He's so irritable; he *snaps* / *whispers* / *stutters* at you if you make the slightest mistake.
5 The audience started *muttering* / *shrieking* / *grunting* with excitement when the singer came on stage.
6 You needn't *moan* / *mutter* / *bellow*; I'm not deaf!
7 It gets on my nerves when children continually *whisper* / *whine* / *stutter* to get their own way.

2 Complete the second sentence so that it means the same as the first.

1 Everything she was saying was untrue.
She was lying ____________________ teeth.
2 I'm not going to say anything.
I'm going to ____________________ shut.
3 The guests criticized the lack of facilities at the hotel.
The guests voiced ____________________ the lack of facilities at the hotel.
4 I can't pronounce this word.
I can't get my tongue ____________________ this word.
5 I'm sure he was lying.
I don't ____________________ word ____________________.
6 Everyone is wondering 'When's the test?'
The question ____________________ lips.

Vocabulary from the lesson

3 Rearrange the words to make sentences.

1 here had remarks I've up her with it to rude .
____
2 to having mess of other death up I'm people's clean sick to .
____
3 written number I've complain of count the I've to times of lost .
____
4 to nothing it that about me done think be it will annoys .
____
5 who nerves listen gets if that on don't my it's people one there's thing .
____
6 radios when me beach mad people their on drives the it play .
____
7 child to being object I treated is a like what .
____
8 moaning so always people are I infuriating who find .
____

4 Complete the text with the words from the box.

anger	chest	fuss	moan	nose	piece	times

Plumbers really get up my (1) __________. They are always promising to come at a certain time and nine (2) __________ out of ten they don't turn up when they've said. And if you dare to kick up a (3) __________ about it, then they never come back at all. I'm getting so fed up with my current plumber that I keep phoning up my friends to vent my (4) __________ and get things off my (5) __________ by having a good old (6) __________ about it. But next time he comes late, I will definitely give him a (7) __________ of my mind.

Dictation

5 **07** Write the text that you hear.

1 ____________________.
2 ____________________.
3 ____________________.
4 ____________________.

4B | Voice complaints

VOICE

1 Complete the sentences with a correct form of the verbs in the box.

break	disguise	echo	fade away
lower	raise	strain	tremble

1 'If you carry on shouting like that, you'll ___________ your voice', she warned.
2 'Is there anyone there?' he yelled. But his voice ___________ through the cave, and then slowly ___________.
3 His voice ___________ as he said goodbye to his old friend for the last time.
4 The speaker had to ___________ his voice so as to be heard over the noise of the plane.
5 When his voice ___________, he had to stop singing in the boys' choir.
6 I didn't want her to recognize me on the phone, so I ___________ my voice.
7 'I don't like being shouted at. Please could you ___________ your voice?' she asked.

REPORTED SPEECH

2 Make reported sentences with the verbs in the box.

deny	refuse	regret	remind
suggest	threaten	~~warn~~	

'You'd better not carry too much money.'
She warned me not to carry too much money.

1 'Don't forget to phone the plumber.'
_______________________________________.
2 'I certainly didn't eat your chocolates.'
_______________________________________.
3 'I wish I hadn't brought so much luggage.'
_______________________________________.
4 'I'll call the police if you don't leave now.'
_______________________________________.
5 'No way am I going to wear those shoes.'
_______________________________________.
6 'It might be a good idea to book tickets.'
_______________________________________.

3 Report the dialogue from the point of view of Mr Patel.

A: Do take a seat, Mr Patel. How can I help you?
B: Well, Mrs Jones, I want to make a complaint about my bank account. I see that I've been charged €75 for going €5 into the red. Is that normal?
A: Yes, I'm afraid it is the bank's policy to charge a standard fee if people go overdrawn.
B: But that's ridiculous! This is the first time I've ever had an overdraft.
A: Well, in that case we can overlook it this time, but you must be careful not to go into the red again, otherwise I'm afraid we'll have to apply the charge.

The bank manager invited (1) ______________________
and asked (2) ______________________.
I told her that (3) ______________________
and said that (4) ______________________.
I then asked (5) ______________________.
She explained that (6) ______________________
______________________.
I protested that (7) ______________________
and pointed out that (8) ______________________.
She agreed (9) ______________________
but stressed that (10) ______________________
otherwise (11) ______________________.

4 Correct four mistakes in the reporting structures.

1 He congratulated me for passing the exam.
2 She requested me to keep my voice down.
3 He recommended that I see a therapist.
4 She admitted to having cheated in the test.
5 I insisted to see the manager.
6 She suggested me to take singing lessons.

4c | A speech problem

Emotional reactions

1 Complete the expressions with the words from the box.

fear	death	down	eyes	laughter	life	loud
mood	surprise	tears	up	worked		

1 I was close to __________ / was trembling with __________ / cried my __________ out.

2 It frightened the __________ out of me / scared me to __________ / took me by __________.

3 I got __________ up / laughed out __________ / roared with __________.

4 It cheered me __________ / got me __________ / put me in a good __________.

2 Which is the odd one out in each group in exercise 1?

3 Complete the story using a suitable expression from exercise 1 (more than one may be possible).

File Edit View Favourites Tools Help Link

I remember the first time I went skiing. I was with a group of friends, all of whom were good skiers, and as I had learned quickly on the beginner slopes they took me up to an intermediate slope on my second day. I looked down at the steep slope in front of me and it (1) ______________. I thought I would never get down. But I gradually built up my confidence and was doing quite well until we suddenly turned a corner and saw a huge tree just in front of us, which completely (2) ______________. I tried to avoid it, but didn't know what to do and ended up flat on my face. My friends (3) ______________, but I wasn't amused. My legs were hurting and so was my pride. I (4) ______________, but I didn't actually cry. And on top of that, I (5) ____________ because my friends seemed to find it so funny, and so I gave them a piece of my mind. At the end of the day they took me to a restaurant for a special meal to (6) ____________, but I decided I would never go skiing again.

Vocabulary from the lesson

4 Match the words and phrases 1–8 in column A to the definitions a–h in column B.

A

1 atrocious
2 grip
3 half-witted
4 impediment
5 precarious
6 strike a chord
7 take someone under your wing
8 unorthodox

B

☐ a to look after someone who is younger or less experienced
☐ b to keep someone very interested in something
☐ c to produce an emotion (such as sympathy) in someone
☐ d very unpleasant
☐ e not following the usual rules or beliefs
☐ f likely to change or become dangerous without warning
☐ g a physical or psychological problem that affects how well someone can do something
☐ h stupid (informal)

Translation

5 Translate the text into your language.

Speech therapists aim to 'give people a voice' by improving their communication abilities. They work with people of all ages who have any kind of speech impediment or communication problem. These may include stammers, loss of speech following a stroke or other brain injury, or speech impediments caused by congenital problems, such as a cleft palate. They may also help children whose speech development is delayed for whatever reason, or work with people who have difficulty eating or swallowing. Speech therapy is a rewarding career and normally entails training for three or four years at university. Speech therapists usually work in a multi-disciplinary team alongside other health professionals such as doctors, nurses, physiotherapists and occupational therapists, as well as sometimes liaising with teachers or social workers.

4D | Speech!

MODAL VERBS 1

1 Complete the dialogue with *must*, *might*, *may* or *could*. More than one may be possible.

A: Was everything OK with my flat while I was away?
B: Yes, fine. There are just a couple of things though …
A: What's the problem?
B: Well, for a start, you (1) __________ have told me you had a dog. It frightened the life out of me when it jumped on me in the middle of the night. I thought there (2) __________ be a burglar in the house!
A: Oh, sorry, didn't I tell you about Rover? It (3) __________ have slipped my mind.
B: And another thing – you (4) __________ have mentioned the alarm. It scared me to death when it went off.
A: What alarm? There's no alarm. Maybe it was a car alarm. Or it (5) __________ have been on the TV?
B: Maybe. But apart from that, everything went fine.
A: Good. But there's something I need to say, actually.
B: What's that?
A: It's my new vase. You (6) __________ at least apologize for breaking it! It was a present from my boyfriend.
B: I didn't break it! It (7) __________ have been Rover.

2 Rewrite the sentences using the word in brackets.

1 I'm thinking of possibly going into acting when I leave school.
____. (*might*)

2 She finally managed to get a leading role in a film.
____. (*able*)

3 It's true that she's not stunningly attractive, but she certainly has talent.
____. (*might*)

4 It was possible for me to go to drama school, but I decided against it in the end.
____. (*could*)

5 There's a possibility she'll be nominated for the Best Actress award.
____. (*could*)

6 Even though the critics didn't like the film, I thought it was brilliant.
____. (*may*)

3 Delete the incorrect alternatives to complete the sentences.

1 My uncle was a brilliantly funny speaker;
a) he could always make people laugh.
b) he could have become a professional comedian.
c) he can't have had a sense of humour.

2 It's lucky we arrived early, otherwise
a) we couldn't get seats.
b) we might have missed the performance.
c) we must have had to queue for hours.

3 It's a pity you didn't tell me it was your birthday, otherwise
a) I could have got you a present.
b) I was able to send you a card.
c) I may have organized a party.

4 It was a shock when she didn't win the award
a) but she could soon get over it.
b) and she couldn't help crying.
c) but she was able to disguise her feelings.

5 The film's already started –
a) we might go home.
b) we might as well go home.
c) we might have gone home.

VOCABULARY FROM THE LESSON

4 Choose the correct alternative, a, b or c, to complete the sentences.

1 The President gave a speech to _____ the new healthcare programme.
a) inaugurate b) innovate c) incubate

2 People turned _____ en masse to hear the President's speech.
a) out b) in c) over

3 'It won't be easy,' he said, 'but we'll give it our best _____.'
a) aim b) push c) shot

4 Ladies and gentlemen, I'd like to propose a _____ to the new health programme!
a) cake b) roll c) toast

4 | Reading

1 Read descriptions of four famous historical speeches. Match the words in italics in column A to the definitions a–d in column B.

A

1 Nelson Mandela's speech at the opening of his trial on charges of *sabotage*, on April 20th, 1964.
2 The *abdication* speech of King Edward VIII of England on December 11th 1936. The king abdicated because it was not constitutionally possible for him to marry a divorced person.
3 President Jawaharlal Nehru's *eulogy* of Mahatma Ghandi on February 2nd, 1948.
4 Winston Churchill's first speech as prime minister to the British *House of Commons* on May 13th, 1940 (the first year of World War II).

B

☐ a a speech at a funeral praising the person who has died
☐ b the part of the UK Parliament consisting of elected representatives
☐ c the resignation of a monarch
☐ d deliberate damage to the property of an enemy or opponent

2 Read the short extracts from famous historical speeches A–D and match the descriptions 1–4 in exercise 1 to the extracts A–D.

3 Match the first lines of the speeches 1–4 to the speech extracts A–D.

1 I would say to the House, as I said to those who have joined this government: 'I have nothing to offer but blood, toil, tears and sweat.'
2 Friends and Comrades, the light has gone out of our lives and there is darkness everywhere.
3 At long last I am able to say a few words of my own.
4 South Africa is the richest country in Africa, and could be one of the richest countries in the world.

4 Label the speakers' intentions 1–7 with the speech extracts A–D.

1 try to inspire solidarity _____
2 denounce injustice _____
3 explain a decision _____
4 warn about difficult times ahead _____
5 promise to work for a better future _____
6 express a sense of loss _____
7 express gratitude _____

5 Choose the correct definition, a or b, for each of the words or phrases below, as used in the speech extracts.

1 succeeded (Extract A)
a) achieved what was planned
b) take over someone's position

2 allegiance (Extract A)
a) loyalty
b) gratitude

3 desolate (Extract B)
a) very sad and lonely
b) comforted

4 mighty (Extract B)
a) powerful and impressive
b) doubtful

5 cherished (Extract C)
a) fought against
b) valued and held passionately

6 buoyancy (Extract D)
a) a questioning attitude
b) a feeling of happiness and confidence

6 What do you think? Which speech did you find ...

1 the most inspiring?
2 the most moving?
3 the most interesting?
4 the least interesting?

Read & listen

7 **08** Listen to Reading 4 *World Famous Speeches* on the CD and read the speech extracts again.

Nelson Mandela

WORLD FAMOUS **SPEECHES**

☐ **A**

______. I have never wanted to withhold anything, but until now it has not been constitutionally possible for me to speak. A few hours ago I discharged my last duty as King and Emperor, and now that I have been succeeded by my brother, the Duke of York, my first words must be to declare my allegiance to him. This I do with all my heart. You all know the reasons which have impelled me to renounce the throne. But I want you to understand that in making up my mind I did not forget the country or the empire, which, as Prince of Wales and lately as King, I have for twenty-five years tried to serve. But you must believe me when I tell you that I have found it impossible to carry the heavy burden of responsibility and to discharge my duties as King as I would wish to do, without the help and support of the woman I love.

☐ **B**

______. I do not know what to tell you and how to say it. Our beloved leader, Bapu, as we call him, the Father of the Nation, is no more … We will not run to him for advice and seek solace from him, and that is a terrible blow, not to me only but to millions and millions of this country. He has gone, and all over India there is a feeling of having been left desolate and forlorn. All of us sense that feeling, and I do not know when we shall be able to get rid of it. And yet together with that feeling there is also a feeling of proud thankfulness that it has been given to us of this generation to be associated with this mighty person. In ages to come, centuries and many millennia after us, people will think of this generation when this man of God trod the Earth and will think of us who, however small, could also follow his path and probably tread on that holy ground where his feet had been. Let us be worthy of him. Let us always be so.

☐ **C**

______. But it is a land of extremes and remarkable contrasts. The whites enjoy what may well be the highest standard of living in the world, whilst Africans live in poverty and misery. … The complaint of Africans, however, is not only that they are poor and the whites are rich, but that the laws which are made by the whites are designed to preserve this situation. … During my lifetime I have dedicated myself to this struggle of the African people. I have fought against white domination, and I have fought against black domination. I have cherished the ideal of a democratic and free society in which all persons live together in harmony and with equal opportunities. It is an ideal which I hope to live for and to achieve. But if needs be, it is an ideal for which I am prepared to die.

☐ **D**

______. …You ask, what is our aim? I can answer in one word: It is victory, victory at all costs, victory in spite of all terror, victory, however long and hard the road may be; for without victory, there is no survival. … But I take up my task with buoyancy and hope. I feel sure that our cause will not be suffered to fail among men. At this time I feel entitled to claim the aid of all, and I say, 'come then, let us go forward together with our united strength.'

Edward VIII

5A | Entrepreneurs

Relative clauses

1 Complete the article with the relative clauses a–h.

The Phone Co-op is one of the UK's fastest growing consumer cooperatives. In the last few years, the company's turnover has increased dramatically (1) ___________. The company has also scored consistently high ratings in terms of return on capital employed, (2) ___________.

A consumer cooperative is a retail firm (3) ___________. Its members provide the sole financial backing for the business. Following cooperative principles, the company also distributes any profits (4) ___________ back to members.

The original aim of the Phone Co-op, (5) ___________, was to make cheaper telephone and internet services available to its customers. However, following consumer demand, the company extended its services to residential customers, and membership, (6) ___________, continues to rise every year.

The company's ethical principles, (7) ___________, are based on the cooperative values of self-help, self-responsibility, democracy, equality, equity and solidarity. The Phone Co-op is also committed to following environmental best practice, (8) ___________.

a that are not re-invested

b that is owned by its members

c which includes improving energy efficiency and using renewable energy resources

d which are very important to both customers and members

e which is the key measure of financial performance

f which is the UK's only consumer-owned telecommunications business

g which makes the company a cooperative success story in terms of growth

h which currently stands at around 20,000 customers

2 Complete the extracts 1–6 from company memos with the phrases in the box.

as a result of which	by which time
in which case	several cases where
the point where	the way in which

1 The demand for our product has reached ___________ it will be necessary to recruit more staff.

2 The national economy is in a recession, ___________ we are now facing the prospect of bankruptcy.

3 We would like to express our appreciation for ___________ staff have worked so tirelessly to meet our production deadline.

4 Our new product range is due to be launched in May, ___________ we hope to have expanded into the Asian market.

5 Investigations have revealed ___________ members of senior management accepted gifts in return for securing a deal.

6 It may become necessary to reduce our workforce, ___________ staff will be offered voluntary redundancy.

3 Mark bad news in exercise 2 with ✗ and good news with ✓.

5B | A new business

SETTING UP IN BUSINESS

1 Complete the table with the phrases 1–9.

1 Start using your investment capital
2 Make sales forecasts
3 Differentiate your product from competitors
4 Design the logo
5 Set out your goals
6 Provide information on your target market
7 Pitch your ideas to investors
8 Agree on percentage equity for investors
9 Source your suppliers

1 Put together a business plan
a) ______
b) ______
c) ______
2 Secure financial backing
a) ______
b) ______
3 Develop a prototype
a) ______
b) ______
4 Develop a brand image
a) ______
b) ______

2 Complete the crossword. Find the mystery word.

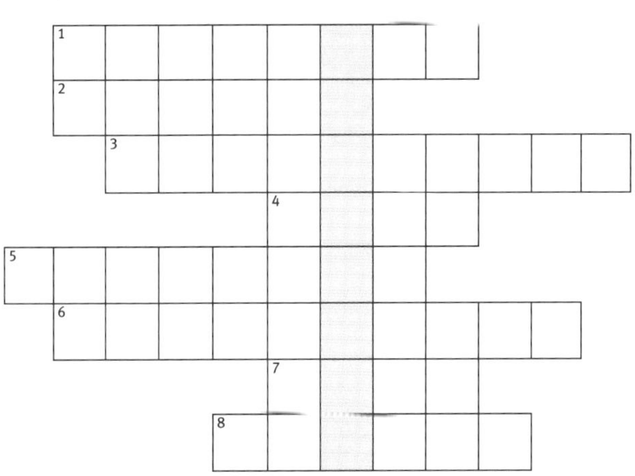

1 A company which provides you with the materials you need to develop a product.
2 The money you get back from an investment.
3 New, original.
4 A business agreement.
5 A prediction about the future.
6 A rival company or product.
7 The image a company uses to market a product.
8 The potential customers for your product.

QUESTION TAGS

3 Complete the utterances with an appropriate question tag.

1 You haven't seen Tony, ______?
2 We'd better go, ______?
3 I'm late, ______?
4 Let's have lunch, ______?
5 The buses are never on time, ______?
6 Answer the phone, ______?
7 Nobody is missing, ______?
8 There's no hurry, ______?
9 Don't tell anyone, ______?
10 Oh, so your name's James Bond, ______?

TRANSLATION

4 Translate the text into your language.

Starting and running your own business is one of the most exciting choices anyone can make. Millions have done so successfully and found it an exhilarating and rewarding challenge. However, it's important to think about all the implications of your decision when starting a business.

You need to seriously consider whether starting your own business is right for you, by honestly appraising your strengths and weaknesses. Do you have the skills and the determination it will require? Do you have the full support of your family and friends?

You should also look very carefully at your circumstances. In almost every instance, starting a business involves a degree of financial uncertainty and risk. Can you afford to forego the stability of a regular wage or salary? Can you afford to lose any of the money or assets you might invest in the business? Are you in a position to wait for revenues and profits to start growing?

______

______

______

5c | Women's work?

Intensifying adverbs

1 Match the groups of adverbs 1–8 in column A to the adjectives they collocate with a–h in column B.

A

1 sorely / bitterly / deeply
2 fully / well / only too
3 strongly / vehemently / fiercely
4 perfectly / quite / fully
5 acutely / deeply / highly
6 highly / fiercely / intensely
7 pitifully / woefully / hopelessly
8 practically / virtually / almost

B

☐ a aware	☐ e embarrassed
☐ b capable	☐ f impossible
☐ c competitive	☐ g inadequate
☐ d disappointed	☐ h opposed

2 Choose one of the adverb-adjective pairs from exercise 1 to complete sentences 1–8.

1 Most men nowadays are ___________ that their partners will expect them to help with the housework.
2 However, some men are still ___________ to the idea of sharing domestic chores.
3 I believe that men are ___________ of doing the ironing if they set their minds to it.
4 He was ___________ to admit that he had no idea how to wash the dishes.
5 Discovering that their husbands or wives are not the ideal partners they had imagined can leave newly-weds feeling ___________.
6 It is ___________ for parents of young children to find time to spend together.
7 The ___________ atmosphere in many firms is uncongenial for some women.
8 Childcare facilities for working women in this country are ___________.

Vocabulary from the lesson

3 Complete the words to match the definitions 1–6.

1 get married (verb, informal)
t_________ the k_________
get h_________
2 the man you will marry
husband-t_________-b_________
3 a newly-wed woman (humorous)
b_________ bride
4 the adjective from *marriage*
m_________
5 the adjective from *wife*
w_________
6 break up (verb)
g_________ your separate w_________

4 Complete the text with the words or phrases from the box.

from bad to worse	from top to bottom
metamorphosis	mismatch
out of character	out of tune

There is often a (1) _____________ between a couple's premarital fantasies about marriage, and the actual reality. June's new husband, for example, refused to do any household duties, which was totally (2) _____________ with her expectations. But instead of letting things go (3) _____________, June threatened divorce. Alarm bells started ringing, and he underwent a complete (4) _____________, behaving in ways that were entirely (5) _____________ – doing the laundry, ironing his shirts, and even cleaning the house (6) _____________. This new division of labour has given a new lease of life to their marriage.

Dictation

5 **09** Write the text that you hear.

5D | Sexual discrimination

Gender

1 Complete the words to describe the jobs in a neutral way.

1 Fire f__________
2 Head t__________
3 Police o__________
4 Flight a__________
5 Sales p__________

2 Replace the words in italics with a less neutral alternative.

1 'I urge you to choose careers which will help you work for the benefit of *humanity*.'
2 'It took over ten *working hours* to put out the blaze.'
3 'If we are to combat crime effectively, then we simply need more *personnel*.'
4 'I think you'll find that these *synthetic* fabrics are more durable than natural ones.'
5 'With four cabin crew off sick, the flight was severely *understaffed*.'

3 Which of the people in exercise 1 may have made the statements in exercise 2?

Hypothetical past situations

4 Complete the second sentence so that it means the same as the first.

1 I wasn't offered the job because I was four months pregnant.
If I __________ four months pregnant, I __________ the job.

2 I couldn't find suitable childcare facilities, so I had to turn down the job. Now I'm still unemployed.
If I __________ suitable childcare facilities, I __________ the job. If I __________ the job, I __________ unemployed now.

3 I was passed over for promotion because I'd filed a complaint for sexual harassment. Now I'm struggling financially.
If I __________ a complaint for sexual harassment, I __________ financially.

4 I couldn't rise to a senior post on account of the glass ceiling.
If it __________ the glass ceiling, I __________ a senior post.

5 As a woman, I was earning 20% less than my male colleagues.
If I __________ a man, I __________ 20% more.

6 When I got back from maternity leave, I found I'd been demoted to a junior position.
If I __________ maternity leave, I __________ a junior position.

5 Complete the sentences to express three different regrets for Sarah and Veronica.

1 Sarah was training as a dentist but, despite advice from her friends and family, gave up her course to have four children in quick succession. Now her children are at school, she is finding it hard to find well-paid work.
a) I wish __________.
b) If only __________.
c) I should __________.

2 Veronica delayed having a family to pursue her career as a lawyer. She went back to work straight after having her son. She now envies her friend Sarah who has four children and spent time with them when they were young.
a) I wish __________.
b) If only __________.
c) I should __________.

5 | Reading

1 Match the jobs 1–7 in column A to their descriptions a–g in column B.

A

1 a bricklayer
2 a carpenter
3 a handyman
4 a labourer (or builder)
5 a plasterer
6 a plumber
7 a stonemason

B

☐ a someone whose job is to fit and repair pipes, water tanks and other equipment used for supplying and storing water
☐ b someone whose job is to put plaster on walls or ceilings
☐ c someone whose job is to build walls using bricks
☐ d someone whose job is to cut stone for building and decorating
☐ e someone whose job involves hard physical work, for example, building work
☐ f someone whose job is to make things from wood or to repair things that are made from wood
☐ g someone whose job is to repair things and do other types of practical work in people's houses

2 Which of the jobs in exercise 1 could not be done by a woman, in your opinion? Why?

3 Which of the following problems do you think female builders might face?

1 The work is too physically demanding.
2 People do not believe they are capable of doing the work.
3 People believe the work is not suitable for women.
4 It is difficult to get training.
5 Building firms prefer to take on male builders.
6 Customers prefer to employ male builders.
7 The work is badly paid.
8 They encounter sexual harassment from men.

4 Read the article and say which of the problems in exercise 3 the women builders have encountered.

5 Find evidence from the article for the following statements.

1 Attitudes to women have been slower to change in the construction trade than in other areas of work.
2 WAMT endeavours to improve working conditions for women.
3 Women who enter the trade nowadays do so for different reasons than they did in the past.
4 It is important to know the right people if you want to find work in construction.
5 One male builder prefers to have female colleagues than male ones.
6 The WAMT director believes that attitudes to female builders will eventually change.

6 Choose the best definition, a, b or c, for the phrases from the article. One of the phrases has two definitions.

1 Twenty at a push
a) less than twenty
b) possibly twenty, but no more
c) twenty or more

2 The odd comment
a) occasional comments
b) strange comments
c) a strange comment

3 Their male counterparts
a) their male colleagues
b) men who do equivalent work
c) their husbands or boyfriends

4 He has no qualms about driving a van.
a) He does not enjoy driving a van.
b) He does not intend to drive a van.
c) He is not worried about driving a van.

5 A tall order
a) an impossible task
b) a difficult task
c) an important task

6 Stand up to the big boys
a) achieve the same standard as men
b) do the same work as men
c) refuse to be treated unfairly by men

7 What do you think? Choose the sentence, 1, 2 or 3, that best matches your opinion and say why.

1 I would prefer to have a male builder to do building work for me.
2 I would prefer to have a female builder to do building work for me.
3 I don't care if the builder is male or female, as long as they do a good job.

READ & LISTEN

8 **10** Listen to Reading 5 *Can she fix it?* on the CD and read the article again.

CAN SHE FIX IT?

Yes she can! As Julie Bindel discovers, female builders are in huge demand – but can they ever compete with the tea-swilling boys?

Of all the construction workers employed at London's Wembley Stadium, what percentage would you guess are women? Five? Ten? 20 at a push? How about 0.05%? 'Out of 10,000,' notes Karen Procter, director of the national organization, Women and Manual Trades (WAMT), 'between three and five are women'. Across the building trade in Britain, women account for fewer than 1% of workers, making the building site still very much a man's domain – what Procter describes as 'the last bastion of sexist discrimination in the workplace'.

Amid all this bad news, though, there are a few success stories. Three years ago, plasterer Janet Shelley set up Women Builders, a company that now employs the UK's largest female construction workforce – fourteen full-time builders. So I set off to meet Shelley and two of her colleagues, Louise Horwood, a 20-year-old carpenter and Lyn Sheridan, 42. Both have encountered some sexist attitudes, and the odd comment like, 'Don't you need to be strong to do that work?' and say that sexual harassment can be bad, but probably 'no worse than working in a professional kitchen'. 'The worst moments,' says Sheridan, 'are when men say to you, "Don't break your nails, love," or, if we are gutting a kitchen, "Shouldn't you be cooking in this, not building it?"'

Before retraining as a plasterer, Shelley worked in IT for fifteen years. 'I decided I needed a radical career change,' she says. After realizing that suitable training courses were rare, she started Women Builders and was immediately contacted by other women. 'We have no problems filling vacancies,' says Shelley. 'There are lots more women wanting to work in the trade than there are jobs.' She works closely with WAMT – which represents and supports women working and training in skilled manual and craft occupations – to try to establish better working practices and reduce discrimination. When WAMT began in 1975, small numbers of middle-class, white, educated women entered the trade partly to protest at women's exclusion. Today, however, 60% of members are black, and have similar class backgrounds to their male counterparts. 'Most of these women are moving out of manual jobs, like cleaning and catering, into trades where they can earn four times as much,' says Procter.

97% of all jobs on building sites are recruited by word of mouth and personal recommendation. Only 3% are advertised, and when women apply, they are often given the cold shoulder. 'One woman rang about a bricklaying job,' Procter says, 'and was asked, "Are you applying on behalf of your husband, love?"' It is not all bad news though. Both Horwood and Sheridan say they get 'a lot of respect' for doing such a hard job, and that there are people who prefer women to men when they need building work done at home, for example, women living on their own.

Given that there are hardly any women builders with the on-site experience to provide training to new recruits, Women Builders employs small numbers of men to do so. Mike Lewis has been with the firm for nearly two years and says he has never been happier. A builder for 23 years, he has no qualms about driving a van with the Women Builders logo. 'I have trained girlfriends in stonemasonry in the past,' he says. 'I love working with women.' Lewis tells me he prefers the atmosphere at Women Builders to the 'competitive' culture that dominates when men get together.

'We are at the stage with women construction workers today that we were 25 years ago with male nurses,' Procter believes. 'In a few years, it will be far more common to see women in hard hats up on scaffolding.' Proportionately, there are more female soldiers and police officers than builders, and part of the reason, Procter believes, is women being told they are not strong enough for the heavy work – something she insists is untrue. Horwood and Sheridan are obviously fit for the job, swinging bags of cement mix with ease. They have the occasional injury, but have never encountered a task they can't manage.

But if women in building are to really flourish, it is crucial to combat the extreme levels of sexism and discrimination in the building trade and see many more women encouraged and trained to work on building sites, alongside men who treat them as equals. A tall order, maybe, but these women certainly know how to stand up to the big boys.

6A | Body care

Nouns from phrasal verbs

1 Complete the phrasal nouns with *out* to match the definitions.

1 exercise session in the gym ______out
2 place where you pay at a supermarket ______out
3 clothes worn for a special occasion out______
4 result (eg of a meeting or discussion) out______
5 a sum of money given to someone ______out
6 beginning out______
7 sudden beginning (eg of war) out______

"THERE WAS A MILD OUTBREAK OF OPTIMISM ALL OVER THE WORLD TODAY.... BUT IT'S NOT EXPECTED TO LAST."

2 Complete the sentences with the phrasal nouns from exercise 1.

1 I knew right from the ______________ that there was going to be a problem.
2 I bought a new ______________ for the wedding.
3 Record profits mean that this year shareholders will receive a massive ______________.
4 Please take the goods to the ______________, sir.
5 The ______________ of fighting left 20 people injured.
6 What was the ______________ of the negotiations?
7 The two-hour ______________ left him exhausted.

3 Complete the sentences with the words and phrases from the box.

bleak heavy in communication of anger poor scientific strict

1 Please ignore his occasional outbursts ___________; I'm afraid he's rather temperamental.
2 The discovery of penicillin was a major ___________ breakthrough.
3 Increasing deforestation means that the outlook for the world's forests is ___________.
4 The talks failed because of a breakdown ___________.
5 We sheltered under a tree when we were caught in a ___________ downpour.
6 We were disappointed by the ___________ turnout at the meeting.
7 I wish my parents had been more lenient with me; I had a very ___________ upbringing.

Vocabulary from the lesson

4 Complete the text with appropriate prepositions.

You don't need to spend two hours running (1) _____ a treadmill if you want to stay (2) _____ shape. Incorporating more physical activity (3) _____ your daily life can be a wonderful way of getting fit and killing two birds (4) _____ one stone. Try going to work (5) _____ foot instead of (6) _____ the underground, for example. Walking (7) _____ a brisk pace can be a wonderful alternative (8) _____ the two-hour ordeal at the gym, and can help you fit regular workouts (9) _____ a busy working week.

Dictation

5 **11** Write the text that you hear.

____
____
____
____

6B | Medical care

Passives 1

1 Complete the sentences with the correct passive form of the verbs in the box.

check	forbid	keep	pay	permit
receive	remind	vacate		

1 Guests __________ that smoking __________ in the bedrooms as this is a fire risk.

2 Noise must __________ to a minimum at all times.

3 Rooms must __________ before 11.00.

4 Electrical appliances must __________ at reception prior to use.

5 Telephone calls may not __________ after 23.00.

6 All items taken from the minibar must __________ for.

7 No alcoholic beverages __________ on the premises. Have a pleasant stay!

2 Rewrite the sentences in the correct passive form, omitting the agent where appropriate.

1 A bee stung him.

______________________________________.

2 An ambulance rushed him to hospital.

______________________________________.

3 Doctors are currently operating on him.

______________________________________.

4 They should have given him an anaesthetic.

______________________________________.

5 Hospital staff are making him stay in bed.

______________________________________.

6 They have warned him to avoid beehives.

______________________________________.

3 Choose the best sentence to follow the first one, using the Given/New rule.

1 Penicillin revolutionized medical treatment.
a) Alexander Fleming discovered penicillin.
b) It was discovered by Alexander Fleming.

2 Penicillin is still used for many bacterial infections.
a) It is not used in cases where patients are allergic to it.
b) Other antibiotics are used in cases where patients are allergic to penicillin.

3 Acupuncture is a form of medicine that has been practised for thousands of years.
a) It is still widely used in Chinese hospitals.
b) Many Chinese hospitals still use it.

4 Needles are inserted into the skin at strategic points.
a) They are sterilized before use.
b) Some patients are anxious about the needles.

Body collocations

4 Match the words 1–10 to their collocations a–j.

1 ear ☐ a teeth
2 empty ☐ b feet
3 rotten ☐ c plugs
4 swollen ☐ d stomach

5 bare ☐ e nose
6 eye ☐ f drops
7 pierced ☐ g feet

8 blocked ☐ h stomach
9 eye ☐ i nose
10 upset ☐ j strain

5 Complete the texts with collocations from exercise 4.

1 Take two spoonfuls twice a day after meals.
Warning: DO NOT take medicines on an __________.

2 **Sore throat?** Coughs and sneezes? __________?
For instant relief from colds and flu, take Cold-eze.

3 **Warning:** to avoid injuries, do not walk in __________ around the swimming pool area.

4 To reduce __________, avoid prolonged staring at a computer screen.

5 Try drinking peppermint tea to calm an __________. Avoid coffee, citrus fruits, fatty foods, onions, alcohol and chocolate.

6 If you are disturbed by noise and have trouble sleeping, why not try **Slumberfast** wax __________?

6c | Taken care of

CARE

1 Rewrite the sentences using the words in brackets.

1 It's completely unimportant to me whether or not I pass the exam.
(*care/less*) ______________________.

2 I hope that people are looking after you well.
(*well/cared*) ______________________.

3 You should pay more attention to your spelling.
(*greater/care*) ______________________.

4 She was singing as if she had nothing at all to worry about.
(*care/world*) ______________________.

5 I hate to think how long I've been working here.
(*care/remember*) ______________________.

6 Remember to look after your money.
(*take/care*) ______________________.

VOCABULARY FROM THE LESSON

2 Complete the definitions with the correct form of the verbs from the box.

fuss huddle overlook pull out
scribble shrug smuggle stamp

1 If you ______________, you write hurriedly and without taking care.

2 If an official ______________ your passport, they put an official mark on it with a rubber instrument.

3 If you ______________ something, you take it out of a country or into another country illegally.

4 If you ______________, you raise your shoulders to indicate that you either don't know or couldn't care less.

5 If people ______________ together, they stand close to each other for comfort or warmth.

6 If you ______________ something, you fail to notice it or decide not to pay attention to it.

7 If a car ______________, it moves away from the pavement into the road.

8 If you ______________ about or over something, you show excessive concern about it, in a worried way.

3 Match the adjectives 1–5 to their collocations a–e.

1 bleak	☐	a	children
2 incessant	☐	b	decision
3 insurmountable	☐	c	prospects
4 irrevocable	☐	d	shelling
5 tearful	☐	e	obstacles

4 Complete the text with the collocations from exercise 3.

When I had made up my mind to adopt Natasha, I knew there was no going back – it was an (1) ______________. With the (2) ______________ and the remorseless sniper fire, there seemed to be (3) ______________ for the future of the besieged city. As we joined the queue of (4) ______________ who were saying goodbye to their mothers, I wondered whether we would be able to get away from the city. There were so many seemingly (5) ______________ that our escape felt impossible.

TRANSLATION

5 Translate the text into your language.

Why are there so many orphans in children's literature? Not only do orphans like Snow White and Cinderella feature in many fairy tales, but they are also the heroes and heroines of modern novels and films. Batman, Harry Potter and Luke Skywalker were all either born orphans or lost their parents at an early age. In classical literature, many orphans struggle in difficult circumstances, but find wealth and happiness at the end of the tale.

Several theories have been put forward to explain the popularity of the literary orphan. Some have suggested that these characters dramatize the powerlessness that children often feel and demonstrate how it is possible to take care of themselves and overcome obstacles against all odds. Another function of the orphan story may be to allow the child reader to think about growing up and leaving home, and reassure them that this will one day be possible.

6D Childcare

Babies & babysitting

1 Complete the notes to a babysitter with the words and phrases from the box.

bib   burp   cot   dummy   feeding bottle   high chair   nappy   pram   pushchair   rattle   teddy bear

Thanks so much for agreeing to babysit Molly!
Here are a few things to remember.
She should have her milk at 4.00.
Her (1) ____________ is in the kitchen, next to the cooker. You can warm it up in the microwave. Remember to (2) ____________ her after you've fed her, by patting her on the back. There is also some baby food in a tin next to the microwave. You'd better put her in her (3) ____________ to feed her, and remember to put her (4) ____________ on, otherwise she'll get food all over her clothes.
If she cries, you'd better check to see whether her (5) ____________ needs changing (there are some disposable ones in the bathroom). If not, try shaking her (6) ____________ to distract her. If all else fails, put her (7) ____________ in her mouth – that usually calms her down.
If you want to take her out, you can put her either in her (8) ____________ or her (9) ____________, both of which are in the garage.
Her bedtime is 8.00. Put her in her (10) ____________, and make sure she has her (11) ____________, as she won't go to sleep without him.
Thanks again – and good luck!!

2 Complete the words and phrases to match the definitions.

1 a fit of anger ta______
2 to shout (informal) ye______
3 argue over small things sq______
4 a child who cries too much cr______
5 to hug affectionately cu______
6 to start crying suddenly bu______ into t______

Passives 2

3 Delete the incorrect alternatives in the text. There may be more than one incorrect answer.

We're off on holiday to France next week, and there's so much to do – I don't know how I'll (1) *have done it all / get it all done / do it all* in time. The major nightmare is the passports – Tom (2) *stole his passport / had his passport stolen / got his passport stolen* on holiday last year and hasn't got round to (3) *having it to be replaced / getting it replaced / having it replaced* yet. And I've just noticed that mine has expired, so that will need (4) *to be renewed / to renew / renewing* too. The car needs (5) *fixing / being fixed / getting fixed*, but there won't be time to take it to the garage so I'll have to (6) *fix it / have it fixed / get it to be fixed* myself. And I'll need (7) *to pack my bags / to have my bags packed / packing my bags*, and then I'll have to (8) *clean the car / have the car cleaned / get the car to be cleaned* by myself …

4 Rewrite the sentences using passive reporting structures.

Zac Goodman is considering transferring to Manchester United, according to rumours in the football world. It is expected that a decision will be announced later today. Goodman allegedly argued with his manager over pay and conditions. Players believe he is unhappy with his pay at Liverpool; some estimate he is currently earning over €80,000 a week. However, he was reportedly offered a six-figure sum by United. Experts consider that Goodman is the best player in British football today.

1 Goodman is rumoured ______________________.
2 A decision is expected ______________________.
3 Goodman is alleged ______________________.
4 He is believed ______________________.
5 He is estimated ______________________.
6 Goodman is reported ______________________.
7 He is considered ______________________.

6 | Reading

1 Match the words 1–8 in column A to their definitions a–h in column B.

A

1 cell
2 clone
3 DNA
4 embryo
5 immune
6 organ
7 tissue
8 transplant

B

☐ a a part of your body that does a specific job, such as your heart or brain
☐ b the smallest part of a living structure that can operate as an independent unit
☐ c a medical operation in which a new organ is put into someone's body. The organ is taken from the body of another person, especially someone who has just died, who is called a donor.
☐ d an animal or human before it is born, when it is beginning to develop and grow
☐ e the substance that animal and plant cells are made of
☐ f an exact copy of an animal or plant created in a laboratory from the animal's or plant's DNA
☐ g safe from a disease, because you cannot be infected by it
☐ h deoxyribonucleic acid: a chemical substance that contains genetic information and is found in all living cells and some viruses

2 Read the text and say where you think it comes from, 1, 2, 3 or 4.

1 A research paper
2 A scientific journal
3 A medical report
4 A popular magazine

3 Choose the best titles a–g for the paragraphs 1–7.

☐ a Fall from grace
☐ b The cloning connection
☐ c Adult stem cells
☐ d Miracle technology?
☐ e Ethical minefield
☐ f ESCs
☐ g What are stem cells?

4 Choose the correct alternative, a, b or c, to complete the sentences.

1 The ESCs used in stem cell technology are produced
a) naturally in the body.
b) artificially in a laboratory.
c) either naturally or artificially.

2 Scientists can stop the body rejecting transplanted tissue
a) by using tissue from donors other than an identical twin.
b) by using ESCs from a clone of the patient.
c) by using an embryo from the patient.

3 Some people object to ESC technology because
a) its benefits have not yet been proved.
b) it is a lengthy process.
c) it involves destroying embryos that are potential human beings.

4 Suk Hwang's work caused controversy amongst scientists because
a) he did not tell the truth about his experiments.
b) he produced the world's first cloned animal.
c) he used ESCs to treat patients.

5 Match the words or phrases highlighted in the text to the synonyms 1–8:

1 able to survive ________
2 complete ________
3 dilemma ________
4 gets round ________
5 obsolete ________
6 obstacle ________
7 troubled ________
8 uncertain ________

6 What do you think? Choose the sentence, 1, 2 or 3, that best matches your opinion and say why.

1 Scientists should be free to develop ESC technology.
2 ESC technology should be banned.
3 ESC technology should be allowed, but subject to regulation.

READ & LISTEN

7 **12** Listen to Reading 6 *Stem cells* on the CD and read the text again.

STEM **CELLS**

1
Fast-forward to the end of the 21st century: surgeons can create new organs to order, regrow crippled spines and hearts, and reverse the damage of Parkinson's disease or diabetes with ease. Immune rejection and waiting lists for replacement organs are consigned to history. Stem cells may have the potential to fulfil this promise and much more, but there are still many technical, ethical and political obstacles to overcome before real therapies are possible.

2
There are two types of stem cell: those found in adult cells and embryonic stem cells (ESCs). Currently, stem cells of both types are being tested to treat many conditions, including: Alzheimer's disease, blood disorders, blindness, deafness, diabetes, heart disease, kidney failure, liver damage, multiple sclerosis, osteoporosis, Parkinson's disease, spinal cord injuries, strokes and cancer. Doctors have been transplanting adult blood stem cells, in the form of bone marrow transplants, for many decades, but stem cells from human embryos were only isolated and cultured in 1998. Though research has progressed rapidly since then, we still have much to understand; not only what gives stem cells their unique properties, but also how exactly they are able to differentiate into the 300 or so different types of human cell in the human body.

3
Embryonic stem cells (ESCs) come from fertilized human embryos just a few days old. In the embryo, these cells go on to form all the tissues of the developing body. They have generated so much interest because they are virtually immortal in the laboratory and are pluripotent, ie they have the potential to turn into many different types of cell, from bones to brain cells. So far, most existing ESCs come from human embryos left over from infertility treatments; however, in some countries women are now donating eggs specifically for stem cell research. The cells could potentially be cultured in the lab as an unlimited source of repair tissue for many ailments, and could be studied to provide vital clues about how the tissues of the body, and certain congenital diseases, develop. They might also be used to test new drugs in the lab instead of on people or animals.

4
The so-called adult stem cells are found in a number of organs in the bodies of both adults and children, including bone marrow, blood, the cornea and retina, intestine, liver, muscles, nervous system and the brain, pancreas and skin. These stem cells are less flexible than ESCs and are typically only able to form cells of the tissue in which they reside; they also suffer from the disadvantage of not being immortal in the laboratory. However, they sidestep the ethical quandary of destroying embryos, and it may be possible to stimulate the adult stem cells we already possess to repair damaged tissues within our bodies.

5
The most significant hurdle still to be surmounted in stem cell technology is immune rejection. As with any tissue transplant (from a donor other than an identical twin), the body will recognize ESCs as foreign and mount an attack which could destroy them. Therapeutic cloning is a clever technique that circumvents this problem. Custom-made ESCs, formed from a patient's own DNA and a donor egg, contain the DNA of the recipient and would not be treated as foreign by the immune system. However, the cloned embryo could in theory be implanted into a womb where it might develop into a cloned human baby. This would be reproductive cloning and is the same method that was used to produce Dolly the sheep, the world's first successfully cloned animal.

6
Producing viable clones of many species is a lengthy and difficult problem and, despite questionable claims of success, has yet to be proven in humans. In any case, reproductive cloning has been banned in many European countries for ethical reasons and because of suspected health risks to the clone. Opponents argue that all embryos, whether created in the lab or not, have the potential to go on to become a fully-fledged human, and therefore it is morally wrong to experiment on them. Other countries have taken the line that the medical benefits outweigh these concerns, and therapeutic cloning has been allowed, although subject to strict regulation. In the United States, disagreement between the religious groups who want a total ban on cloning and an equally vociferous pro-therapeutic cloning lobby has currently stalled legislation on stem cell technology.

7
Politics is not the only controversy that has dogged the stem cell world. In May 2005, one of the world's top stem cell scientists – South Korea's Woo Suk Hwang – announced that his team had used therapeutic cloning to produce ESCs tailored to individual patients. This was one of a string of remarkable achievements. In 2004 Hwang cloned human embryos for the first time, and he later produced the world's first cloned dog – an Afghan hound named Snuppy. Then in late 2005, the research community was rocked by claims that much of his research had been fabricated. The repercussions travelled far and wide, and the already controversial field of stem cell research was brought further into disrepute. It remains to be seen how much the scandal will delay the development of the miracle therapies that are so desperately desired.

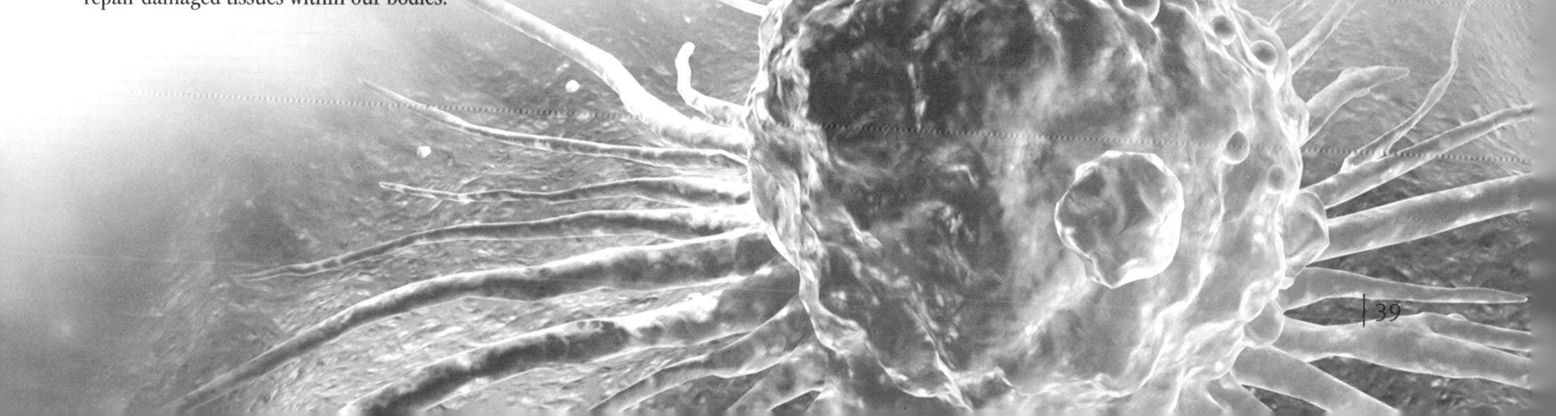

7A | Behaving badly

Vocabulary from the lesson

1 Complete the sentences with words that mean the opposite of those in italics.

1 I'd much rather go to a *single-sex* school than a ___________ one.
2 In my school, the discipline is very *relaxed*; I'd hate to go to a school where the discipline is more ___________.
3 Are you in favour of *traditional* teaching methods, or more ___________ ones?
4 The teachers at my primary school were really *strict*, but the ones at my secondary school were much more ___________.
5 It helps when pupils are *keen* on learning; if they are ___________ and unmotivated, they tend not to make much progress.
6 Unfortunately, teachers have to spend so much time dealing with ___________ pupils that the *well-behaved* ones often get ignored.
7 She sends her children to a ___________ school because she doesn't believe in *private* education.
8 Teachers nowadays tend to be a lot more *easy-going* than they were when I was young; we used to find our teachers very ___________.

2 Complete the sentence beginnings with a preposition.

1 He's hoping to put his feet __________
2 He came in to turn the school __________
3 If a school is __________ the brink of shutdown,
4 I caught a glimpse __________ two students
5 The boy who set __________ the fire alarm
6 We need to get a grip __________ truancy
7 The private schools that are springing __________ everywhere
8 Strict punishments will be handed __________

3 Match the sentence beginnings 1–8 from exercise 2 to the endings a–h.

☐ a to pupils caught in acts of misbehaviour.
☐ b was severely punished by the headmistress.
☐ c because discipline had broken down.
☐ d and relax when he retires.
☐ e bear witness to the failure of state education.
☐ f the staff and pupils have to pull together to improve standards.
☐ g if the school is to escape closure.
☐ h embroiled in a fight in the playground.

4 Underline the punishment that is more lenient.

1 get suspended / get a detention
2 pick up litter / get excluded
3 get caned / stay behind after school
4 get expelled / get suspended
5 get let off with a warning / get reported to the police
6 the softly-softly approach / corporal punishment

Ellipsis

5 Complete the sentences using an elliptical verb form, as in the example.

My brother Henry and I have nothing in common …

1 He has a good job but *I haven't*.
2 At school he always got good marks but __________.
3 He used to like studying but __________.
4 He never got punished but __________.
5 He's been to university but __________.
6 He earns a lot of money but __________.
7 He doesn't have to work hard but __________.
8 His children are well-behaved but __________.
9 He's happy but __________.

6 Delete any unnecessary words in the dialogue, substituting where appropriate.

Example:

A: Did Sammy set the fire alarm off?
B: No, Sammy didn't set it off – Jamie set it off. (1) *No, Sammy didn't – Jamie did.*
A: Where's Jamie? Has he gone home? (2) __________________.
B: He might have gone home. Will he be punished, do you think? (3) __________________.
A: He deserves to be punished, but he probably won't be punished. The pupils at that school can get away with anything. (4) __________________.
B: The pupils in my son's school can get away with anything too. One swore at the teacher but the teacher didn't do anything. (5) __________________.
A: He should have done something. Otherwise children lose all respect for authority. (6) __________________.
B: They've already lost respect for authority. (7) __________________.
A: I've complained to the head teacher. Have you complained? (8) __________________.
B: I would complain if I thought it would do any good. (9) __________________.

7B | Rudeness

Good & bad behaviour

1 Complete the sentences so that they have the same meaning as the phrases in italics.

1 The man *swore* at his grandmother.
He used f__________ l__________.

2 He was *very careful to say and do the right thing, so as not to cause offence.*
He was on his b__________ b__________.

3 They *stood in a line and waited patiently* to be served.
They formed an o__________ q__________.

4 My neighbours *dance and play loud music with their friends* until the small hours.
They have r__________ p__________.

5 He always *observes a strict code of etiquette when he is eating.*
He has good t__________ m__________.

6 She *was punished severely* for her misbehaviour.
She g__________ into serious t__________.

7 I can't stand *the way some fans are rude and violent at football matches.*
I can't stand the l__________ behaviour of some football h__________.

Vocabulary from the lesson

2 Complete the email with a correct form of the words and phrases from the box.

feel grumpy	go on at	have a row
put himself in	put up with	take it out on

File Edit View Favourites Tools Help Link

I've just (1) ______________ with my dad about good manners. Honestly! He's always (2) ______________ me to improve my manners, but he's a fine one to talk! Whenever he's in a bad mood, or (3) ______________, he (4) ______________ me, as if it was my fault! Why should I have to (5) ______________ his abusive behaviour? Instead of having a go at me, he should (6) ______________ other people's shoes, and try to be a better role model himself!

Ellipsis in conversation

3 Delete any words that are not needed in the questions.

1 **A:** Is anybody sitting here?
B: No, it's free.
A: It's a lovely day, isn't it?
B: Yes, beautiful.
A: Do you mind if I smoke?
B: Go ahead.
A: Have you got a light?
B: Haven't, I'm afraid.
A: Would you like a cigarette?
B: No thanks. Don't smoke.
A: Is this your first time in Paris?
B: No, I've been here loads of times.
A: Well, it was nice talking to you. I hope to meet you again sometime …

2 **A:** Are you ready yet?
B: Almost. Just need to do a few more things. Won't be a minute.
A: Is there anything I can do?
B: That would be very helpful. Is there any chance you could phone for a taxi?
A: Sure, no problem. I'll do it straight away.

3 **A:** Are you busy at the moment?
B: Yes, very busy. I'm revising for my exams. What about you?
A: I'm busy too. Spent the whole of the weekend studying.
B: Do your teachers give you a lot of homework?
A: Yes, loads. Never get a chance to relax …

'No! Don't jump in that muddy puddle! You haven't got your best clothes on!'

Dictation

4 13 Write the text that you hear.

____

____

____

____

7c | Whodunnit?

Vocabulary from the lesson

1 Rearrange the upper case letters to form the names of different kinds of books.

1 FLES-PHEL ____________
2 EARLYRIT SLICCAS ____________
3 CREMONA ____________
4 HIPARUGABOYTO ____________
5 MERIC ELVON ____________
6 TOPYER ____________

2 Match each book 1–6 from exercise 1 to the blurb extracts a–f.

☐ a This magical collection sparkles with originality; the images and sounds harmonize in a thoroughly satisfying manner.

☐ b The inside story of one of the last century's most successful artists; poignant, witty and intensely engaging.

☐ c ... aims to show readers how to improve their motivation, cope with unfair criticism and set goals for themselves.

☐ d ... an exciting and superbly-structured plot and vivid evocation of place. A subtle and powerful work of contemporary fiction that keeps you on the edge of your seat right to the end.

☐ e ... and sensitive characterization. A beautifully written book about love, jealousy and betrayal.

☐ f A new translation of one of the world's best-loved novels, with an introduction by Howard Mills.

Participle clauses

3 Say whether the function of the participle clause is to denote (more than one may be possible):

1 an action happening just before another.
2 an action happening at the same time as another.
3 a cause.
4 a result.

☐ a He threw a brick at the window, making a hole large enough to get through.

☐ b Looking nervously behind him, he broke into the safe.

☐ c Removing the money, he ran off.

☐ d Hearing the alarm go off, they ran towards the safe.

☐ e Not having been present at the scene of the crime, I was unable to assist the police with their enquiries.

☐ f Having taken fingerprints from all the suspects, the forensic scientist went to process the evidence in the lab.

☐ g Puzzled by this new piece of evidence, he sat down to reflect.

☐ h He frowned, wondering what to do next.

4 Correct ten mistakes in the article.

A car being parked on the corner of West St and Haywood Rd was broken into last night at 11.35pm. A local resident, Mrs Edith Bailey, spotted a man ageing between 18 and 25 years old while breaking into the car. He smashed the car window, setting off the alarm. Because seeing the man was carrying a gun, she did not approach him, having preferred to phone the police. Being late at night there were no other witnesses. Arriving at the scene of the crime, the police checked the car for fingerprints and sealed off the area.

The police speaking on local radio, they have issued a description of the youth having been seen breaking into the car, and have appealed to the public to come forward with any information about anyone who is matching the description. They have warned that the youth is armed and may be dangerous. If being seen, he should not be approached. With more and more cars having been stolen in the area in recent months, they have also advised the public to be extra vigilant about car security.

7D | Crime reports

Vocabulary from the lesson

1 Complete the crossword. Find the mystery word.

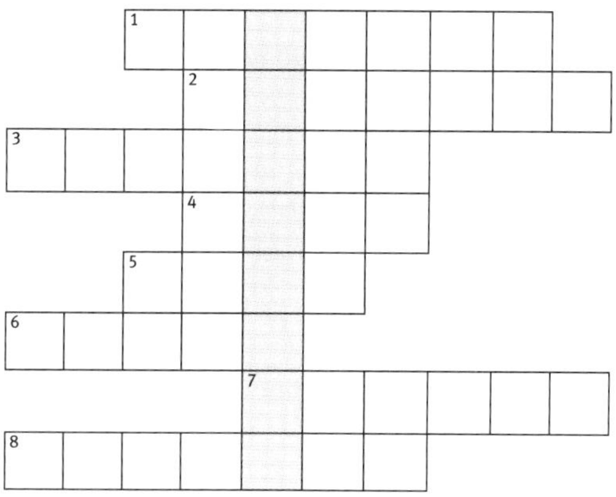

1 A physical attack on someone or the crime of physically attacking someone.
2 An official judgement made in a court.
3 The act or habit of staying away from school without permission.
4 To kill or hurt someone by pushing a knife or other sharp object into their body.
5 A statement that someone makes in a court.
6 The illegal use of fire to destroy a house, building or property.
7 To do (something illegal or morally wrong).
8 The crime of giving money or presents to someone so that they will help you by doing something dishonest or illegal.

Legal matters

2 Complete the sentences with the correct preposition. Then rearrange the sentences in each group in a logical chronological order.

1 ☐ a He went on trial __________ fraud.
☐ b He was charged __________ fraud.
☐ c He was jailed __________ six years.
☐ d He was found guilty __________ fraud.
☐ e He was sentenced __________ a six-year jail term.
☐ f He was arrested __________ suspicion of falsifying documents.

2 ☐ a She appealed __________ the sentence.
☐ b She pleaded not guilty __________ arson.
☐ c She was accused __________ setting fire to the school.
☐ d She was convicted __________ arson.
☐ e She was cleared __________ the offence.
☐ f She was put __________ trial.

3 Rewrite the sentences with the words or phrases from the box.

charges	convictions	a fine
a life sentence	a plea	a verdict

1 'I plead not guilty', said Fraser.
Fraser ______________________________.
2 Fraser had been convicted of burglary several times in the past.
Fraser ______________________________.
3 'You must pay €400', ordered the judge.
The judge ______________________________.
4 'We no longer accuse you of theft', said the police officer.
The police ______________________________.
5 'I find you guilty', declared the judge.
The judge ______________________________.
6 'You must remain in prison indefinitely', said the judge.
The judge ______________________________.

Translation

4 Translate the text into your language.

Criminology can be defined as the study of the nature, causes and consequences of crime. It draws on a range of academic disciplines, including sociology, law, psychology, economics, biology and statistics in order to shed light on questions such as why people commit crimes, what is the best way to deal with criminals, and how crime can best be prevented. Traditionally, it was thought that criminals were born bad; now we understand that the reasons why people turn to crime are complex, and are related just as much to society as to individuals.

Criminologists have been influential in the reform of prisons and the judicial system. Their research has shown, for example, that prison makes people more, not less, likely to offend; and that innovative schemes such as restorative justice (whereby criminals have to confront their victims) can be a powerful means of preventing reoffending, as well as an effective form of rehabilitation for many young offenders.

As regards crime prevention, criminologists have shown that increasing the size of the police force does not necessarily make the streets more safe. They have also highlighted the huge incidence of fraud (the so-called 'white collar crime'), which costs countries' economies billions of dollars every year.

____

____

____

7 | Reading

1 Match the definitions 1–8 to the crimes from the box.

robbery murder manslaughter
receiving stolen goods attempted murder
assault criminal trespass rustling

1 physically attacking someone __________
2 trying intentionally to kill someone (though not succeeding) __________
3 stealing livestock, eg cows, sheep __________
4 accepting another person's property while knowing that it was taken illegally __________
5 causing someone's death illegally but unintentionally __________
6 stealing something by using force or threatening to use force __________
7 entering a place without the owner's permission __________
8 killing someone intentionally __________

2 Read Text A. List the crimes in exercise 1 that are mentioned and the punishment given for each one.

rustling – transportation to Australia on a convict ship

3 Read Text B. Choose the best subtitle 1–4 for Texts A and B.

Text A ☐
Text B ☐

1 Fact or fiction?
2 Outlaw, robber and murderer
3 A success story
4 Champion of the poor and oppressed

4 Choose the best alternative, a or b, to complete the sentences about Text B.

1 Tenant farmers sometimes stole livestock because
 a) they sometimes did not have enough to eat.
 b) they resented the fact that their landlords were wealthy.

2 Ned's father was imprisoned because
 a) he could not afford to pay £25.
 b) he attempted to steal a young cow.

3 After his father's death, Ned Kelly
 a) frequently got into fights with the police.
 b) decided to stand up for the rights of others.

4 Fitzpatrick
 a) assaulted members of Ned's family.
 b) was later found to be untruthful.

5 At Stringybark Creek
 a) Ned asked the policemen to lie on the ground.
 b) Ned attempted to spare the policemen's lives.

6 During the bank robberies, Ned
 a) tried to publicize his view of events.
 b) was shot and badly injured.

5 Why did the writers of Texts A and B include the expressions in italics below? Match each expression 1–8 in column A to the reason a–h in column B.

A

1 (Text A) Ned Kelly was *the son of an Irish convict.*
2 (Text A) Ned stole the watch of a man he had murdered, *asking cynically, 'What's the use of a watch to a dead man?'*
3 (Text A) The *infamous* siege was a ploy by the Kelly Gang to trap the police.
4 (Text B) Ned was constantly in trouble with the police *for minor offences.*
5 (Text B) Kelly never harmed his hostages, but *on each occasion he gave one of them a letter.*
6 (Text B) Ned was found to be wearing *a green bloodstained sash that he had been given during his childhood for rescuing a drowning man.*
7 (Text B) Despite *a petition signed by thirty thousand supporters* Kelly was hanged.
8 (Text B) He was *just twenty-five years old.*

B

☐ a to emphasize the criminal motives behind the gang's actions
☐ b to highlight Ned's brave and noble character
☐ c to make the readers feel sorry that Ned had a short and tragic life
☐ d to suggest that Ned's main motivation was to seek justice for himself and others
☐ e to show Ned's widespread popularity with ordinary people
☐ f to show that criminal tendencies run in families
☐ g to suggest Ned Kelly was a cold and heartless villain
☐ h to suggest that Ned's crimes have been exaggerated

6 Which opinion, 1, 2, 3 or 4, do you agree most with?

1 Ned Kelly was a villain who deserved the death penalty.
2 Ned Kelly was a hero who fought for the poor.
3 Ned Kelly was a victim of circumstance whose life shows how social conditions can lead to a life of crime.
4 It's hard to know the true facts behind the lives of people who have become national heroes.

READ & LISTEN

7 **14** Listen to Reading 7 *The Life of Ned Kelly* on the CD and read the texts again.

THE LIFE OF NED KELLY

Text A

Edward (Ned) Kelly was born in 1854, the son of an Irish convict who had been transported to Australia in the first convict ships after being found guilty of stealing two pigs from a neighbour. Ned's criminal career started at the age of fourteen, when he was arrested for assaulting a local pig farmer; and following a further charge of assault a year later, he was sentenced to three months' hard labour on each count. Three weeks after his release, Kelly was imprisoned for three years for receiving a stolen horse; and in 1878, he was convicted in his absence of the attempted murder of a policeman and sentenced to a further fifteen years' imprisonment.

Together with other members of the notorious 'Kelly Gang', Ned then went into hiding in the Australian bush. It was here that the gruesome murder at Stringybark Creek took place, when Ned shot dead three policemen who tried to arrest them. As he left the crime scene, Ned stole Sergeant Kennedy's gold watch, asking cynically, 'What's the use of a watch to a dead man?' Following the killings, the lawless Kelly gang were involved in two major bank robberies, leading to Kelly being declared an outlaw who could be shot on sight without arrest or trial. However on 26th June 1880, the same day their outlaw status expired, Dan Kelly and another gang member went to the house of a police informer and shot him in cold blood.

Ned Kelly's final confrontation with the police came during a shoot-out at the famous Glenrowan Inn where the gang, dressed in heavy metal armour, took about seventy hostages, two of whom were fatally shot. The infamous siege was a ploy by the Kelly Gang to trap the police and use them as hostages to secure the release of Ned's mother, Ellen, from prison. After a foiled attempt to derail the train carrying the police force to the inn, Kelly was arrested, sentenced to death on three counts of murder, and finally hanged on 11th November 1880.

Text B

Ned Kelly was born into a large and impoverished family of tenant farmers in Australia. Scraping a living from small plots of land with poor soil, and at constant risk of eviction by their landlords, these farmers were sometimes forced to resort to stealing livestock from their wealthy landlords, simply in order to survive. When Kelly's father, Red, was tried for stealing a calf, he was acquitted of the crime but found guilty of removing the brand from the calf's skin and fined £25. As he was unable to pay the fine, he served six months' hard labour; however, his health did not survive the harsh conditions in jail, and he died when Ned was just twelve.

After this experience, Ned vowed to fight for justice for the poor and oppressed people in his community. This set him on a collision course with the authorities, who were widely seen as corrupt, and as a young man he was constantly in trouble with the police for minor offences and sometimes beaten up by them. After serving three years' hard labour for receiving a stolen horse (a crime of which Ned maintained his innocence throughout his life), he discovered on his release that all but one of his thirty-two horses had been stolen by the local police force.

Not long after this, a police officer named Fitzpatrick accused Ned's mother of attacking him and Ned of shooting him in the wrist. Kelly always protested his family's innocence, insisting he was away in a different province at the time; nevertheless, his mother was imprisoned, and he was convicted of attempted murder on Fitzpatrick's unsupported evidence (Fitzpatrick was later dismissed from the police force for drunkenness and perjury). Ned escaped to the bush with his brother Dan and, while he was in hiding at Stringybark Creek, he met three policemen whom he believed were intending to kill him. He offered them the chance to surrender but, when they did not lay down their firearms, he shot them. From then on, Ned was a wanted man, with an £8,000 reward offered for his capture.

During this time the Kelly Gang robbed two banks. Kelly never harmed his hostages, but on each occasion gave one of them a letter denouncing the corruption of the police and their persecution of his community, and calling for justice for the poor and the release of those who had been wrongfully imprisoned. He was finally shot and badly wounded during the Glenrowan siege where, under his armour, he was found to be wearing a green bloodstained sash that he had been given during his childhood for rescuing a drowning man. After a hurried trial, and despite a petition signed by thirty thousand supporters, he was hanged in November 1880 on three counts of murder. He was just twenty-five years old.

8A | It takes all sorts

Noun phrases

1 Match the phrases from the box to the photos A–F.

a bottle of lemonade   a coffee cup   leopard skin
a leopard's skin   a cup of coffee   a lemonade bottle

A

D

B

E

C
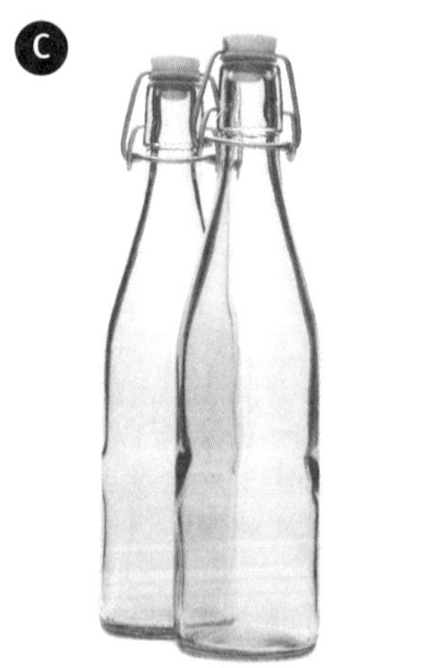

F

2 Match the words and phrases 1–10 to the nouns a–j.

1	suede	☐ a	rocking chair
2	oak	☐ b	knife
3	stainless steel	☐ c	boots
4	cardboard	☐ d	coat
5	fur	☐ e	table
6	mahogany	☐ f	box
7	pine	☐ g	slippers
8	porcelain	☐ h	wardrobe
9	straw	☐ i	jug
10	sheepskin	☐ j	basket

3 In exercise 2, find ...

1 three things to wear in cold weather.

____

2 three items of furniture.

____

3 two things to use in a kitchen.

____

4 two containers.

____

4 Complete the sentences with noun phrases formed from the words in brackets.

1 They sell cheap (*men, shirts*) at the (*stall, clothes*) at the (*open air, market, Wednesday*).
2 We had a (*discussion, next week, lessons*) at (*yesterday, meeting, staff*).
3 I left my (*key, front door*) on the (*kitchen table*).
4 My (*neighbour, next door*) works as a (*presenter, quiz, show*) on (*breakfast, television*).
5 I got the (*six o'clock, bus*) and it was a (*one hour, journey*) to the (*airport, city*).
6 Although she is a (*woman, great intelligence*) she unfortunately seems to lack a (*sense, humour*).
7 I read an interesting (*article, language, learning*) in (*Sunday, edition,* the Times).

Vocabulary from the lesson

5 Complete the text with the words from the box.

blurred   bursting at the seams   ill-assorted
rambling   rickety   skimpy   skinny

This is a photo of me in my first student flat – it's a bit (1) __________, I'm afraid. I'm the one in the (2) __________ T-shirt and shorts. I can't believe I was so (3) __________ in those days. I've put on quite a bit of weight since then, as you can see! I was living in a(n) (4) __________ old house with a(n) (5) __________ bunch of people – students, artists, musicians. The house was (6) __________ with (7) __________ old furniture – you could hardly move around!

Dictation

6 **15** Write the text that you hear.

____

____

____

8B | Birth order

Character traits

1 Match the words 1–8 in column A to the descriptions a–h in column B.

A

1 obsessive
2 easygoing
3 ruthless
4 rebellious
5 single-minded
6 down-to-earth
7 conscientious
8 outgoing

B

☐ a Once Hannah has decided to do something, she puts all her energy into achieving her goal.
☐ b If you tell Kate to do one thing, she'll do the opposite, just to defy you.
☐ c Ed has a very practical attitude to life – he's not one of those types who always have their head in the clouds.
☐ d Amy just can't think or talk about anything apart from clothes.
☐ e Gareth doesn't care who he hurts or upsets as long as he can get his own way.
☐ f Dan is always relaxed and never loses his temper, even if you provoke him.
☐ g You can rely on Nathalie – she puts a lot of hard work and effort into whatever she has to do.
☐ h Tom's the life and soul of the party – he loves socializing and making new friends.

2 Delete the incorrect alternatives.

My eldest brother Simon is a rather impulsive (1) *nature / type / attitude* – he has a (2) *sense / tendency / streak* to act hastily. And he has quite a competitive (3) *streak / tendency / type* too – he was always trying to beat me at games. Mark is the second child and I think he was always in Simon's shadow – he suffers from a(n) (4) *streak / lack / attitude* of confidence, and has a(n) (5) *tendency / attitude / sense* to act more cautiously. My younger sister Carrie, on the other hand, has a very happy-go-lucky (6) *sense / tendency / attitude* to life and a great (7) *sense / attitude / nature* of fun. And me? I keep the peace between all of them and try to sort out their differences!

Vocabulary from the lesson

3 Complete the text with the words and phrases from the box.

astrology attitude birth order determine
gender genetics life events sibling relationships

There are a number of different factors which influence or even (1) __________ an individual's personality. Some people argue that 'nature' has the most influence, especially (2) __________, ie inherited characteristics, as well as (3) __________ – that is, whether a person is male or female. Others argue that differences are mainly due to 'nurture', or cultural and environmental influences. These include the (4) __________ and behaviour of parents; (5) __________, ie a person's position in the family; (6) __________, where someone is not an only child; and (7) __________ such as illnesses or successes. Finally, there are those who believe that (8) __________ has a large role to play, and that personality is greatly affected by the stars.

4 Match the descriptions 1–6 in column A to their opposites a–f in column B.

A

1 She tends to mimic what the rest of her family do.
2 She's a non-conformist by nature.
3 She has a tendency to fuss over details.
4 She's always acting the fool.
5 She never loses her temper.
6 She has a rather cautious nature.

B

☐ a She's always very laid back.
☐ b She's an unconventional type and likes to do her own thing.
☐ c She has a real sense of adventure and likes to take risks.
☐ d She's rather stroppy, always finding fault and getting into arguments.
☐ e She takes life very seriously.
☐ f She doesn't like to rock the boat.

Translation

5 Translate the text into your language.

According to a recent survey, friendship is in something of a decline. Twentysomethings have on average between six and fourteen friends and lifelong friendships are becoming a thing of the past. But it is not just the quantity of friends that is changing. Sadly, it seems that even the quality of our friendships is becoming strained. Many people nowadays tend to prioritize work over close relationships, or lose touch with old friends when they move away to a new town. However, it is important to work at and nurture our friendships and make an effort to stay in touch even when people move away. After all, apart from our immediate families, our friends are the most important people in the world.

8c | A close bond

Relationships

1 Put the text in the correct order. The first one has been done for you.

- ☐ extended family. I do think it is important to try to build a good
- ☐ terms with my immediate
- ☐ relations with other countries.
- ☐ breakups and families who are not even on speaking terms with each other. And on a local level I think it's important to foster close
- ☐ relationships in the past with members of my
- *1* I'm generally on very good
- ☐ links with one's neighbours and build a sense of community. Politicians can help to set a good example by maintaining good diplomatic
- ☐ rapport with one's friends and family, especially nowadays when there are so many marriage
- ☐ family but I have had some stormy

Attitude adverbials

2 Choose the best alternative to complete the sentences.

1 She's just had a blazing row with her father, and *not surprisingly / funnily enough / miraculously*, she's feeling pretty upset.

2 We used to be very close but she moved to a different town and *ironically / inevitably / to my amazement*, we drifted apart.

3 I don't know why so many young people nowadays see so little of their parents. *Undoubtedly / Certainly / Surely* we have a responsibility to look after them as they get older?

4 It was my birthday yesterday, and *much to my amusement / to my great delight / somewhat to my disappointment*, none of my friends remembered.

5 We're best friends now, but *worryingly / oddly enough / predictably* we didn't get on when we first met.

6 A good friendship is *surely / wisely / undoubtedly* one of life's great blessings.

3 Complete the extract of a letter with the words and phrases from the box.

clearly	foolishly	incredibly	quite rightly	sadly	understandably

... As for the family, well there have been a few developments. As you know, Ben and Alexa got married three years ago but (1) _______ it didn't work out, and they split up at the beginning of the year. Ben spent nearly all his time at work, or playing golf with his friends at weekends and (2) _______ Alexa wasn't prepared to put up with it. She (3) _______ told him that he would have to make more of a commitment to the marriage if they were to stay together. But (4) _______ he wasn't ready for a serious relationship, and left. I (5) _______ said to her that there were plenty more fish in the sea, but this just made her more upset. (6) _______, I think she still hopes he'll come back. Not much chance of that, I'm afraid ...

Vocabulary from the lesson

4 Match the phrases 1–6 in column A to their dictionary definitions a–f in column B.

A

1 agonize over something
2 dump someone
3 let go of something
4 take to someone
5 rely on someone
6 turn to someone

B

- ☐ a to begin to like someone
- ☐ b to go to someone for help when you are having difficulty dealing with a situation
- ☐ c to stop holding something
- ☐ d to trust someone to do something for you
- ☐ e to spend a long time worrying and being upset about something
- ☐ f to get rid of someone that you no longer want or need

8D | Singles

Discourse markers

1 Complete the table with the discourse markers in the box.

as a rule | that is to say | at least | by the way | incidentally | even so | generally speaking | to put it another way | mind you | quite honestly | to be frank | actually

1 **Make a general statement**	4 **Invite or admit honesty**
______ ______	______ ______
2 **Clarify or explain**	5 **Change the subject**
______ ______	______ ______
3 **Show contrast**	6 **Limit, modify or correct**
______ ______	______ ______

2 Choose the best alternative to complete the sentences.

1 It's hardly surprising he can't stay in a relationship. *Incidentally / After all / At least*, he doesn't know how to compromise.
2 There's no point criticizing her for staying single. It's her choice, *to put it another way / as a rule / ultimately*.
3 I miss my boyfriend now we've split up. *Still / In fact / After all*, there are plenty more fish in the sea.
4 He's glad his wife walked out on him. That's what he says, *to be frank / anyway / even so*.
5 He doesn't do much around the house. *In fact / Mind you / Still*, he's bone idle.
6 Married life certainly has its advantages. *In fact / Ultimately / Mind you*, it's not a bed of roses all the time.

3 Put the sentences in the correct order in each text.

a ☐ For one thing, I'm too busy.
☐ And anyway I've seen it three times already.
☐ On top of that, I've got a bit of a headache.
☐ I don't really want to go and see the film.

b ☐ To start with, it's too noisy and polluted.
☐ We've decided to move out of the city.
☐ Besides, we just can't afford to buy a house in the city centre.
☐ For another thing, we fancy living in the country for a while.

Adverbs with two forms

4 Match the verbs 1–10 to the adverbs a–j to make collocations.

1 play music ☐ a lightly
2 sleep ☐ b widely
3 take things ☐ c loudly
4 travel ☐ d hard
5 try ☐ e easy

6 aim ☐ f short
7 cut things ☐ g light
8 go to bed ☐ h out loud
9 laugh ☐ i high
10 travel ☐ j late

5 Complete the sentences with the adverbs from the box.

easily | hardly | highly | lately | shortly | wide

1 If you'll take a seat, I'll be with you ________.
2 Have you read any good books ________?
3 She is keen and ________ motivated to improve.
4 I'm not asleep, I'm ________ awake!
5 ________ anyone works as hard as I do.
6 Don't talk to him, he's ________ distracted.

8 | Reading

1 Read the extract from the classic novel *Pride and Prejudice*, written by the English author Jane Austen and first published in 1813. Choose the best title for the extract, a, b, c or d.

a A happy engagement
b A marriage proposal
c An angry confrontation
d A declaration of mutual love

2 Match the words from the extract (some are in a different form) 1–5 to those which have a similar meaning a–e.

1 astonishment	☐	a	composure
2 agitation	☐	b	anxiety
3 apprehension	☐	c	disturbance
4 exasperation	☐	d	amazement
5 calmness	☐	e	anger

3 Decide whether the statements about the extract are true (T) or false (F). Underline evidence from the text to support your answers.

1 Elizabeth was not expecting Mr Darcy's visit. _____
2 Elizabeth encouraged Mr Darcy to start the conversation. _____
3 Mr Darcy declared his love for Elizabeth. _____
4 Elizabeth had suspected that Mr Darcy was in love with her. _____
5 Elizabeth felt flattered by Mr Darcy's words to her. _____
6 Mr Darcy had tried to change his feelings towards Elizabeth. _____
7 Mr Darcy expected Elizabeth to accept his proposal. _____
8 Elizabeth accepted his proposal. _____

4 Answer the questions with *E* (Elizabeth), *D* (Mr Darcy) or *B* (both Elizabeth and Mr Darcy).

1 Who found the other person's words surprising?
2 Who had a mixed reaction to the other's words?
3 Who felt annoyed by the other person?
4 Whose skin changed colour?
5 Who felt sure of receiving a particular answer?
6 Who found it hard to remain calm?

5 Match the formal phrases 1–10 from the extract in column A to their modern equivalents a–j in column B.

A

1 My feelings will not be repressed.
2 You must allow me to tell you how ardently I admire and love you.
3 In such cases as this, it is, I believe, the established mode to express a sense of obligation for the sentiments avowed.
4 however unequally they may be returned.
5 I have never desired your good opinion,
6 I am sorry to have occasioned pain to anyone. It has been most unconsciously done.
7 I hope will be of short duration.
8 And this is all the reply which I am to have the honour of expecting
9 But it is of small importance.
10 I might, perhaps, wish to be informed why, with so little *endeavour* at civility, I am thus rejected.

B

☐ a I know I should be flattered that you feel like this.
☐ b I'm crazy about you.
☐ c Anyway, it doesn't matter.
☐ d I hope you soon get over it.
☐ e I don't care what you think of me.
☐ f What's wrong with me?
☐ g I can't hold my feelings in any more.
☐ h I don't feel the same about you.
☐ i I didn't mean to hurt you.
☐ j Is that all you can say?!

6 What do you think? Choose the sentence(s) that best matches your opinion, 1, 2, 3 or 4, and say why.

1 Mr Darcy's proposal was insulting to Elizabeth.
2 Elizabeth reacted too rudely to Mr Darcy.
3 Elizabeth should have accepted Mr Darcy's proposal.
4 Mr Darcy was right to express his feelings honestly.

READ & LISTEN

7 **16** Listen to Reading 8 *Pride and Prejudice* on the CD and read the extract again.

Pride & Prejudice

Elizabeth Bennet, the second of a family of five daughters, has recently made the acquaintance of Mr Darcy, a wealthy gentleman with a large estate. He does not make a favourable impression on Elizabeth, who finds him proud and condescending, and her family are his inferiors in terms of class, money and social manners. One day, Mr Darcy arrives at the Bennet family's house.

Elizabeth was suddenly roused by the sound of the door-bell and, to her utter amazement, she saw Mr Darcy walk into the room. In a hurried manner he immediately began an inquiry after her health; she answered him with cold civility. He sat down for a few moments and then, getting up, walked about the room. Elizabeth was surprised, but said not a word. After a silence of several minutes, he came towards her in an agitated manner, and thus began:

'In vain I have struggled. It will not do. My feelings will not be repressed. You must allow me to tell you how ardently I admire and love you.'

Elizabeth's astonishment was beyond expression. She stared, coloured, doubted and was silent. This he considered sufficient encouragement; and the avowal of all that he felt, and had long felt for her, immediately followed. In spite of her deeply-rooted dislike, Elizabeth could not be insensible to the compliment of such a man's affection; and though her intentions did not vary for an instant, she tried to compose herself to answer him with patience. He concluded with representing to her the strength of that attachment which, in spite of all his endeavours, he had found impossible to conquer; and with expressing his hope that it would now be rewarded by her acceptance of his hand.

As he said this, she could easily see that he had no doubt of a favourable answer. He spoke of apprehension and anxiety, but his countenance expressed real security. Such a circumstance could only exasperate farther, and, when he ceased, the colour rose into her cheeks, and she said:

'In such cases as this, it is, I believe, the established mode to express a sense of obligation for the sentiments avowed, however unequally they may be returned. It is natural that obligation should be felt, and if I could feel gratitude, I would now thank you. But I cannot – I have never desired your good opinion, and you have certainly bestowed it most unwillingly. I am sorry to have occasioned pain to anyone. It has been most unconsciously done, however, and I hope will be of short duration.'

Mr Darcy, who was leaning against the mantelpiece with his eyes fixed on her face, seemed to catch her words with no less resentment than surprise. His complexion became pale with anger, and the disturbance of his mind was visible in every feature. He was struggling for the appearance of composure, and would not open his lips till he believed himself to have attained it. At length, with a voice of forced calmness, he said:

'And this is all the reply which I am to have the honour of expecting! I might, perhaps, wish to be informed why, with so little endeavour at civility, I am thus rejected. But it is of small importance.'

Glossary
civility *n* politeness
It will not do *phrase* It is no use
ardently *adv* strongly
avowal *n* expression
insensible to *v* unaware of
endeavours *n pl* attempts
acceptance of his hand *phr* agreeing to marry him
countenance *n* face
established mode *n* usual custom
sentiments avowed *phrase* feelings expressed
bestowed *pp* given
occasioned *pp* caused

9A | A place called home

Modal verbs 2

1 Match the sentences 1–8 using *will* in column A to the grammar explanations a–h in column B.

A

1 Close the door, will you?
2 The tournament will be held in Spain next year.
3 I doubt whether United will win.
4 I've tried telling him, but he won't listen.
5 On Sundays I'll often get up late.
6 I'll email you when I arrive.
7 He will leave all the lights on!
8 (*Doorbell rings*) That'll be Fred.

B

☐ a annoying behaviour
☐ b future fact
☐ c habitual behaviour
☐ d intention
☐ e prediction
☐ f present assumption
☐ g refusal
☐ h request

2 Delete the incorrect alternatives (more than one may be possible).

1 *Will / Shall / Would* I give you a hand with the washing up?
2 I *will / shall / would* do it myself, but I don't have time at the moment.
3 I didn't bring an umbrella because I really didn't think it *will / shall / would* rain.
4 *Will / Shall / Would* you pass the salt, please?
5 He *will / shall / would* occasionally go jogging on Sunday mornings.
6 Sorry I'm late – the car *won't / shan't / wouldn't* start.

3 Rewrite the sentences using the modal verb in brackets.

1 How about getting a DVD out?

______________________________? (*shall*)

2 He refuses to eat his vegetables.

______________________________. (*won't*)

3 I can't stand the way she's always grumbling about everything.

______________________________. (*will*)

4 He often used to drop by and see us.

______________________________. (*would*)

5 I'm not surprised she caused trouble – that's so typical of her.

______________________________. (*would*)

6 Can you suggest a time for us to meet?

______________________________? (*shall*)

7 I suggest you don't mention it to your father.

______________________________. (*wouldn't*)

8 I expect she's gone to bed by now.

______________________________. (*will*)

Vocabulary from the lesson

4 Match the words 1–8 to the definitions a–h.

1 alleviate	☐ a follow a course that curves a lot
2 amble	☐ b in many parts of a place
3 choked	☐ c spend time in a relaxed way
4 dotted	☐ d make a short visit to
5 draw up	☐ e make something less severe or serious
6 drop by	☐ f prepare and write
7 while away	☐ g walk in a slow relaxed way
8 wind	☐ h filled so that it is hard to move

5 Complete the article with a correct form of the words from exercise 4.

The City Council has (1) __________ a plan for a major new leisure park, to try to (2) __________ some of the problems caused by stress and the pressures of urban living. It will be located on the outskirts of the town, far away from the noise and pollution of the traffic- (3) __________ city centre. A central feature of the plan is a series of (4) __________ paths through woodland where joggers can stop and exercise at strategic exercise points (5) __________ along the route, or where families can simply (6) __________ to (7) __________ a quiet Sunday afternoon. As well as a sizeable sports and leisure complex, there will also be a Fitness Advice Centre where people can (8) __________ for a quick consultation on finding a fitness routine that suits them.

9B | Squatters

Describing homes

1 Complete the labels of the photos.

1 A t________ c________

4 A l________ building

2 A p________ house

5 A l________ c________

3 A d________ house

6 A b________ of f________

2 Match the words 1–7 in column A to the definitions a–g in column B.

A

1 cosy
2 cramped
3 draughty
4 gloomy
5 overgrown
6 rickety
7 threadbare

B

☐ a covered with plants that have been allowed to grow in an uncontrolled way
☐ b a structure or piece of furniture that is likely to break if you put any weight on it, often because it is old
☐ c a place that is uncomfortable because cold air blows into it
☐ d clothing, carpet or cloth that is very thin and almost has holes in it because it has been worn or used a lot
☐ e warm and comfortable, and making you feel relaxed
☐ f dark in a way that makes you feel sad or a little afraid
☐ g small and crowded

3 Match the extracts from estate agents' blurbs 1–6 in column A to the interpretations a–f in column B.

A

1 Ideal for the DIY enthusiast
2 **Natural and mature gardens**
3 Conveniently located for commuting
4 Features a charming 18th-century well
5 Exciting opportunities for decoration
6 Featuring antique furniture

B

☐ a No running water
☐ b Overlooking the motorway
☐ c In urgent need of repair
☐ d Rickety chairs and threadbare carpets
☐ e Overgrown and run-down
☐ f Needs several coats of paint

Vocabulary from the lesson

4 Put the text in the correct order. The first one has been done for you.

☐ the property up, leaving it in a better condition than before.
☐ out by the Squatters Advisory Service. Massive rises in property prices, along with the numbers of families queuing
☐ property values down. However, the reverse is often true and squatters who settle
☐ on the property ladder, and so many turn to squatting. The common perception is that squatters in the neighbourhood bring
☐ up for social housing, have made it increasingly difficult for first-time buyers to get
[1] The number of squatters in the UK has risen dramatically, according to a new survey carried
☐ down in a property for an extended period of time often do

Dictation

5 17 Write the text that you hear.

____

____

____

9c | A place in the sun

Inversion

1 Find and correct ten mistakes in the letter.

Dear Sir,

I am writing to complain about my recent holiday with Sunshine Tours. Every time I travel with your company does something go wrong. Not only we had problems with the flight, which was delayed by four hours, but also was the hotel room extremely noisy. No sooner we arrived than bulldozers started clearing the land right outside my window. Only by keeping the windows shut day and night I could get some sleep, and always had I to sleep with earplugs. Furthermore was the hotel room extremely filthy. Not only had the bathroom not been cleaned adequately, but also had the sheets not been changed on the bed. Only when had I complained three times to the manager was some action taken. I am afraid that never again I will travel with your company.

Yours faithfully,

A Blenkinsop

Agnes Blenkinsop

2 Complete the second sentence so that it means the same as the first.

1 We enjoyed our holiday and also felt we were helping to protect the environment.

Not only ______________________________.

2 I have rarely enjoyed such breathtaking views.

Rarely ______________________________.

3 We arrived, and immediately lunch was brought up to our room.

Hardly ______________________________.

4 They employ only local staff.

Only ______________________________.

5 Disturbing the turtle nests is strictly forbidden.

Under no circumstances ____________________.

6 It is only on this island that tourists can enjoy the benefits of ecotourism.

Only on this island ____________________.

Vocabulary from the lesson

3 Complete the words 1–4 and match them to the photos A–D.

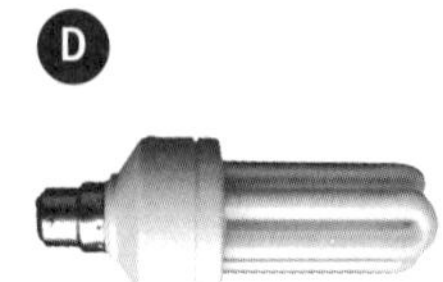

1 r__________ i__________

2 o__________-g__________ produce

3 e__________-s__________ lightbulbs

4 s__________ heating

4 Rearrange the upper case letters to make words.

Excessive tourist development is causing (1) SOONIRE on the beaches, wildlife is being (2) SCIPADDLE by large hotel complexes, and sea pollution is affecting the (3) VOOLISHIELD of local fishermen. Ecotourism is a concept that attempts not only to provide an enjoyable holiday, but also (4) IZEMMINI the impact of tourism on the environment. In this way it sets out to (5) ADAGRUFES the environment and (6) LINTISL in holidaymakers a sense of concern for their surroundings.

Translation

5 Translate the text into your language.

Freshfield House is a century-old thatched cottage situated in a quiet village overlooking the River Errey. Having recently undergone extensive restoration, the property has four bedrooms, two bathrooms, a fully-stocked kitchen, living room, dining room and sun-room/laundry room in approximately 800 square metres. The house can accommodate up to eight guests, with parking for three vehicles. The extensive gardens surrounding the house include an outdoor sitting and dining area, with views across the river to the Medbourne Hills. All areas of the house have been recently decorated and are furnished in traditional style. Recent upgrades include a new boiler and radiators in each room, dishwasher, and cable television. Conveniently located in the heart of the picturesque Freshfield Forest, the local shops are within easy walking distance.

9D | Experimental travel

Vague language

1 Complete the dialogue with the phrases from the box.

and everything	kind of	loads of stuff
or anything	or somewhere	
stuff like that	that sort of place	

A: Hey, nice to see you! You're looking well. Would you like a coffee (1) ______________?

B: Thanks. White, no sugar, please.

A: So, how was your holiday?

B: Great! I did (2) ______________: travelled around, went sightseeing, lay on the beach, that kind of thing.

A: Where did you stay?

B: Mostly youth hostels or cheap hotels, (3) ______________.

A: What do they eat over there? Is the food very spicy?

B: Not really spicy, but very tasty. Lots of fish, seafood, vegetables, (4) ______________. What we ate a lot of was 'empanadas', which is a (5) ______________ pie with meat or seafood or cheese. Cheap and very filling!

A: Sounds really good. I'd like to do something like that. Take time to see a place, get to know the people, the culture, the way of life (6) ______________.

B: Come with me next summer! We can go to Asia – Thailand, Laos, Cambodia (7) ______________.

A: Sounds great! You're on!

Adjectives formed with particles

2 Match the words 1–10 to the words a–h to make collocations.

1 online ☐ a flight
2 outdoor ☐ b struggle
3 overnight ☐ c banking
4 uphill ☐ d swimming pool

5 faraway ☐ e activities
6 indoor ☐ f critic
7 oncoming ☐ g countries
8 outspoken ☐ h vehicle

3 Complete the sentences with a particle.

1 The museum was really fascinating; interactive quizzes, hands-_____ exhibits, things like that.
2 I'd much rather stay in an _____-of-the-way location than in a built-_____ area.
3 We nearly had a head-_____ collision as we were coming down the mountain road.
4 The locals mostly buy made-_____-measure suits rather than _____-the-peg ones, because they're so cheap over there.
5 With the local shops all closing down, you often need to go to an _____-of-town superstore to get what you're looking for.
6 Sometimes we had buffets, but usually the hotel served sit-_____ meals.
7 They bought a run-_____ cottage and did it up – it's really beautiful now.

4 Complete the text with the phrases from the box.

comfortably off	cheesed off	fed up with
hard up	up to date with	worn out

I'm ready for a holiday! I've been working so hard recently, with overtime and working through lunch hours and everything, that I'm really (1) ___________. The problem is, things move forward so fast in my field of work that you have to put in a lot of effort if you want to keep (2) ___________ modern developments. But to be honest, I'm getting (3) ___________ my job; it's not well-paid so I'm a bit (4) ___________ at the moment. I wish I could afford a decent car, a nice holiday, things like that. I asked my boss for a rise but he refused point blank. That really made me feel (5) ___________, especially when I look at most of my friends who are earning decent salaries and are pretty (6) ___________ now. I'm thinking of switching careers and looking for a better-paid job.

9 | Reading

1 Decide which of the items in the box you would expect to find in a slum in Mumbai.

beggars	chickens and goats	criminal gangs
hardworking people	luxury hotels	recycling
factories	squalor	thriving businesses	tourists

2 Read the article and check your answers to exercise 1.

3 Find evidence in the article to support these statements.

1 Conditions in the slums in Mumbai are unhygienic.
2 The walking tours help slum-dwellers.
3 The slums in Mumbai have a reputation for crime.
4 Participants in the walking tours are not always allowed to stop and look around.
5 The streets in the slums are narrow.
6 The slums are a dark place.

4 Match the definitions 1–6 to the highlighted words in the article.

1 strong currents of air, wind, heat, etc __________
2 something that is popular or fashionable for only a short time __________
3 to spend time in a place waiting or doing nothing __________
4 to meet and talk to someone who is important or famous __________
5 to move close together in order to stay warm, feel safe or talk __________
6 large containers for holding or storing liquids __________

5 Read these reactions to Reality Tours. Tick the ones you agree with and say why.

☐ 1 I am not in favour of these tours. It is the worst kind of voyeurism – taking tourists to gape at the poor as if they were animals in a zoo, and exploit their misery.

☐ 2 I think this kind of tour could be a real eye-opener. It seems like a dignified way in which the tourists can get a glimpse of the reality of daily life of the slum-dwellers, with a guide who knows the reality first-hand. It is a good way of dispelling the myths and going beyond the stereotypes and clichés.

☐ 3 When I go on holiday, I want to see beauty and inspirational sights. I would never go on a depressing tour like this.

☐ 4 Poverty is a fact of life. But most people in the West have never experienced real poverty. Maybe it would help them realize just how lucky they are.

☐ 5 Tours like this focus on the negative and just reinforce the stereotype that developing countries are places of poverty and squalor.

☐ 6 If people in the slums are supportive of these tours, and if the profits go to the slum-dwellers, then I see nothing wrong with these tours.

READ & LISTEN

6 **18** Listen to Reading 9 *Alternative tourist trail: Slumming it in Mumbai* on the CD and read the article again.

ALTERNATIVE TOURIST TRAIL:

SLUMMING IT IN MUMBAI

It sounds like the latest travel fad for cosseted Westerners. But tours of India's poorest districts are not only putting money in the pockets of slum-dwellers, but also highlighting their plight. Justin Huggler reports.

The sign was just around the corner from Leopold's, Mumbai's most famous bar, where the Western backpackers rub shoulders with well-off young locals in designer T-shirts. 'Reality Tours and Travel,' it said. 'See the biggest slum in Asia'. It seemed an unlikely offer, guided walking tours of slums so notorious that the average Mumbai citizen is too terrified to set foot in them. Places of legendary squalor, where armies of rats can suddenly fill the narrow lanes, and if you don't look where you're going, you can easily slip into an open sewer. But that is just what a young Briton, Chris Way, is doing. The 31-year-old got the idea for the tours on a trip to Rio de Janeiro. 'I went on a favela tour, which I found very interesting, but I felt that it was nothing compared to the activity and energy of the slums of Mumbai.'

But the tours are about more than making money from a tourist attraction. For one thing, 80 per cent of the profits go to a charity that helps slum-dwellers. 'We want to help change perceptions, both in India and internationally, that the slums in Mumbai are simply places of squalor,' said Mr Way, who makes most of his money from more conventional tours. 'In fact, they're full of hard-working, humble people.' Most startling, he adds that the main slum on his tours, Dharavi, a place with a reputation for poverty, is actually home to a thriving economy, with an annual turnover of £350m. There are even textile businesses that export cloth to the US.

So I decided to join one of Mr Way's tours. First stop was a quick tour through Mahim slum, one of the countless illegal slums that are perched on every empty spot of land in Mumbai. The houses huddle so close together the sound of the street seems distant. Chickens and goats wander freely through the lanes, in the middle of one of the world's biggest metropolises. Then, abruptly, we turn a corner and we are in the light again, the other Mumbai, the world of cars and permanent buildings and money, and the slum is just a huddle of huts behind us. And then we move on to Dharavi, the biggest slum in Asia. Spread over 432 acres, it is home to more than a million people.

Immediately we are in another world. Tiny streets wind like tunnels through buildings packed so close together you can hear the sounds of two televisions competing with each other from houses on either side of the street. Blasts of air hit you from either side: hot air from a bakery, cool air from someone's fan. The 'houses' are one room where a family of ten crowds together. In-between are tiny shops, no bigger than an automated photo booth, where the shopkeeper sits under shelves of groceries. This is a city within a city – and in this neighbourhood, it is a city in perpetual night. Because the buildings meet overhead, no light can penetrate, which makes it feel like you are underground.

You cannot help feeling like an intruder in these residential neighbourhoods: there is little privacy in the slums, and every open doorway lets onto a family's entire home. Mr Way is careful to stress that his tours are not designed to invade the slum-dwellers' privacy. Tourists are asked not to take photographs except in particular areas where the locals have agreed, and not to hang about in some places, but to walk straight through.

But the tour is not about these dark residential tunnels so much as the business quarters of the slum, where Riaz Khan's soap factory is one of the highlights. Mr Khan recycles waste soap from commercial soap factories and sells it as cheap soap for washing clothes. We also visit a biscuit factory, the textiles quarter, and an entire recycling quarter, full of workshops where labourers are beating the dents out of old oil cans and the streets are lined with huge vats of tiny bits of chopped-up computer circuit boards, floating in water before they are recycled. 'This is what we want to show, that the common perception in India, that Dharavi is just a place of criminals, is wrong,' says Krishna Pujari, Mr Way's Indian business partner. 'This is a place of thriving legitimate business.'

10A | Achieving the impossible

Success

1 Complete the sentences with the prepositions from the box. There are two that are not used.

ahead	down	in	off	on	over	out	up

1 That's John. He was always very ambitious – a very keen sportsman. Everyone said he'd get _____ well in life. Now he's an _____-and-coming politician.

2 Lucy always did well _____ exams, always top of the class. Now she's a university professor of economics.

3 Mike – he wasn't an academic high-flier, but he was single-minded and worked hard. In the end his hard work paid _____ and he's got his own IT business now.

4 That's me – very promising at school, everyone said I had a bright future _____. But it didn't turn _____ so well for me – I became a struggling musician.

2 Match the sentence beginnings 1–6 in column A to the endings a–f in column B.

A
1 Doing a project well gives a great sense of
2 Unless you work hard you don't stand a
3 He was finally able to fulfil his
4 He soon rose to the top and is now a high-
5 She is currently director of a thriving
6 Very few people become an overnight

B
☐ a chance of succeeding.
☐ b clothes retail company.
☐ c success – it takes time and determination to achieve your aim.
☐ d ambition of flying a plane solo.
☐ e achievement.
☐ f flier in a multinational finance company.

Vocabulary from the lesson

3 Complete the sentences with the adjectives from the box.

benign	ensuing	euphoric	indelible
long-standing	meticulous	relentless	spellbound

1 Sorry I can't make tomorrow's meeting – I have a(n) __________ engagement I need to keep.
2 The fans were totally __________ when their team won the championship, cheering wildly and embracing each other.
3 I'll never forget our first meeting – it has left a(n) __________ impression on me.
4 Looking at the __________ expression on his face, it was hard to believe that just a moment ago he had been exploding with anger.
5 The president was arrested on corruption charges, and in the __________ trial more facts were revealed about his dealings with foreign governments.
6 On top of her poor health, the __________ pace of work meant that Katherine felt increasingly stressed.
7 The children sat totally __________ as they watched the puppet show.
8 As a result of his lengthy and __________ research, new theories have been formulated.

4 Complete the sentences with the correct preposition.

1 He is obsessed __________ planes, and hopes to become a pilot one day.
2 John Lennon Airport is named __________ one of the city's most famous residents.
3 The stunning new building made everyone stop __________ their tracks.
4 I object __________ being kept waiting by journalists.
5 Because of tight new customs regulations, it is now rare for anyone to be waved __________.

Dictation

5 **19** Write the text that you hear.

____

____

____

____

10B | What is success?

FUTURES

1 Choose the correct alternatives to complete the sentences.

a **A:** What (1) *are you doing / do you do* after the course?
B: I (2) *'m going / 'll go* back to Sweden for the summer then I (3) *might / will* take a holiday. After that (4) *I do / I'm doing* a doctorate in the States. My course (5) *starts / is starting* in October, so I hope I (6) *'ll have had / 'll have* time to do enough reading by the time the course (7) *starts / will start*. And you?
A: I aim (8) *to finish / finishing* my project before July. Then I think I (9) *'m taking / 'll take* a holiday too.

b **A:** (10) *Are you doing / Do you do* anything tonight?
B: No – why?
A: Do you fancy (11) *going / to go* out for a meal around 7.00ish?
B: I'd love to but 7.00 is a bit early – I'll still (12) *do / be doing* my English homework. But I (13) *should finish / should have finished* by 8.00, so we could meet then if you like.

c The CD is (14) *due / on the point* to be released next month. We've had good pre-release reviews, so we're hopeful (15) *of having / to have* good sales. It's (16) *unlikely / bound* to be an overnight success, though, as it takes a lot of time to get known. But with any luck, in a few months from now the song could well (17) *ride / be riding* high in the charts.

2 Underline the event that is more probable, a or b.

1 a) She might win a medal.
b) She may well win a medal.

2 a) I'm thinking of taking up yoga.
b) I'm going to take up yoga.

3 a) You'll get the job.
b) You should get the job.

4 a) I'm watching a film tonight.
b) I'm planning to watch a film tonight.

5 a) There's bound to be a test.
b) There's likely to be a test.

6 a) I anticipate pulling off the deal.
b) I hope to pull off the deal.

3 Complete the sentences using an appropriate future form.

1

2

3

THREE-PART PHRASAL VERBS

4 Rewrite the sentences with three-part phrasal verbs using the verb in brackets.

1 Let me take you out to compensate for missing your birthday.
________________________________. (*make*)

2 You'll get punished for cheating if they find out.
________________________________. (*not get*)

3 I don't know how you tolerate being spoken to like that.
________________________________. (*put*)

4 The government is going to take strict measures to deal with anti-social behaviour.
________________________________. (*crack*)

5 You'll just have to accept the fact that achieving success will be an uphill struggle.
________________________________. (*face*)

6 Are you planning to enter the competition?
________________________________. (*go*)

7 My grandfather was my role model.
________________________________. (*look*)

8 What do you think is the reason for your success?
________________________________. (*put*)

10c | Going wrong?

Weather

1 Match the words 1–10 to their collocations a–j. Join the words to make one where appropriate.

1	flash	☐	a	bolt
2	thunder	☐	b	stones
3	hail	☐	c	beam
4	snow	☐	d	flood
5	sun	☐	e	flake
6	sweltering	☐	f	downpour
7	rain	☐	g	drift
8	torrential	☐	h	drop
9	snow	☐	i	gale
10	howling	☐	j	heatwave

2 Write the word from exercise 1 that is being described in each sentence.

1 As I drew back the curtains, it came shining in through the window, falling on to my bed in a pool of golden light. ____________________

2 Astonishingly, each one is totally unique – a miraculous design of nature. ____________________

3 A total lack of rainfall and temperatures over 35 degrees every day led to a severe water shortage.

____

4 I ran for shelter as they suddenly came crashing down on to the pavement. One was the size of a golf ball.

____

5 I watched it roll down the window pane, like the tears I felt inside. ____________________

6 It kept me awake all night, rattling the windows and causing extensive damage to trees across the region.

____

Vocabulary from the lesson

3 Choose the correct word, a, b, c or d, to complete the sentences.

1 Simon studied the controls on the ________ of his car and tried to work out where to switch on the radio.
a) dashboard b) windscreen c) indicator d) lever

2 We watched the balloon ________ upwards until it disappeared out of sight in the clouds.
a) swoop b) seize c) soar d) sink

3 A woman who was attacked as she walked home from the shops said she feared for her life during her forty-minute ________.
a) ordination b) ordinance c) ordeal d) order

4 As the train came out of the tunnel, I caught my first ________ of the sea.
a) glimmer b) gloom c) glimpse d) glare

5 The pilot is responsible for adjusting the flight path in the light of the situation as he sees it from the ________.
a) bearpit b) cockpit b) fleapit d) pulpit

6 The new high-speed-trains will now ________ along at speeds of up to 300 kph, completing the journey in less than two hours.
a) hurtle b) hurl c) toss d) flail

Translation

4 Translate the text into your language.

This morning it will start frosty everywhere, especially in rural areas, and any mist or cloud should slowly clear through the morning. It will be dry with some prolonged sunny spells, but it will feel much colder, with temperatures falling below zero on higher ground. It will remain dry overnight with mostly clear skies, allowing a fairly severe frost to form. Some mist or freezing fog may develop, so motorists should beware of patches of ice on the roads. Tomorrow there is a strong chance of rain throughout the country, with torrential downpours bringing a danger of flash floods in places. The outlook for the weekend is more snow, with fierce blizzards forecast for the north.

10D | A stabbing incident

MODAL VERBS 3

1 Choose the correct alternatives to complete the email.

… The highlight of the trip was an afternoon spent white-water rafting down a local river. Luckily we (1) *didn't need to bring / needn't have brought* our own equipment because everything was provided: helmets, paddles and life jackets. We (2) *should have brought / must have brought* waterproof clothing though, because we got absolutely soaked as we went down the river. We (3) *had to do / should have done* an hour's training beforehand, which turned out to be essential when we were on the river. Obviously, anyone who couldn't swim (4) *wasn't allowed to go / didn't have to go* on the trip. I must admit I was a bit apprehensive beforehand, but I (5) *needn't have worried / didn't have to worry* because it was an absolutely wonderful and unforgettable experience — you (6) *should try / need to try* it sometime!

2 Find two correct sentences and correct the incorrect ones.

1 Need we to pay in advance?
2 It's 2.00 now and it takes two hours to get there, so if you leave now you must be there by 4.00.
3 You don't have to smoke in here – it's a no-smoking area.
4 I told her she must pay more attention.
5 You mustn't have been so rude to him.
6 You must see that film – it's fantastic!
7 You needn't to bring food – I have some.

NOT TURNING OUT WELL

3 Match the sentences 1–6 in column A to the expressions a–f in column B.

A

1 It was impossible to make further headway with our investigations.
2 The CD sold only a few copies.
3 The company lost so much money that it had to stop trading.
4 There was no way anyone was ever going to be able to remedy the situation.
5 Our efforts to stop the tent blowing down were in vain.
6 The conference was badly organized and chaotic.

B

☐ a It was a flop.
☐ b It didn't do any good.
☐ c It was a total shambles.
☐ d It went bankrupt.
☐ e We drew a blank.
☐ f It was a lost cause.

4 Complete the sentences with a suitable verb.

1 Unless you train harder, you won't ________ it to the final.
2 If my plans to become a lawyer ________ through, I'll retrain as a plumber.
3 You'd better proceed tactfully or the negotiations will ________ to grief.
4 It will be a shame if all your hard work and effort ________ to nothing.
5 You really ought to concentrate harder, or you'll ________ a mess of the painting.
6 I doubt whether their relationship will ________ out – they're just too different.

10 | Reading

1 You are going to read an article entitled *Oscar Pistorius: the fastest man on no legs*. Before you read, look at the photo and note down possible answers to the questions below. Then read the article to check your predictions.

1 Which sport do you think Pistorius practises?
2 In what way could he be *the fastest man on no legs*?
3 Why could able-bodied athletes accuse him of unfair competition?

2 Choose the title that best summarizes each paragraph 1–6, a or b.

	a)	b)
1	a) A difficult choice	b) Promise of success
2	a) First steps to success	b) Record-breaking performances
3	a) Amazing technology	b) A natural solution
4	a) A legal defeat	b) A sporting controversy
5	a) Olympic achievements	b) True sportsmanship
6	a) An unclear future	b) Rethinking disability

3 Decide whether the statements about the article are true (T) or false (F). Underline evidence from the text to support your answers.

1 Oscar's family played an important part in his early success. _____
2 Oscar started running to help improve his skills in rugby. _____
3 In 2008 he won three gold medals in the Olympic Games. _____
4 Some people say the blades allow him to increase his speed by 25%. _____
5 Oscar was banned from using his blades in 2008. _____
6 He is now eligible to compete against able-bodied rivals. _____
7 He believes that fulfilling your potential is more important than winning races. _____

4 Match the highlighted words 1–8 from the article in column A to the definitions a–h in column B.

A

1 pinnacle (para 1)
2 prowess (para 3)
3 undeterred (para 5)
4 wrangling (para 5)
5 quest (para 5)
6 prestigious (para 5)
7 uncharted (para 6)
8 aspiring (para 6)

B

☐ a unexplored
☐ b great skill or ability
☐ c hoping and trying to be successful
☐ d the highest or most successful part
☐ e continuing to do something despite a lack of support or success
☐ f lengthy and angry argument
☐ g a long and difficult search
☐ h admired and respected

5 Match the verbs 1–8 to the nouns a–h from the article to make collocations.

1 confer
2 expend
3 contest
4 face

☐ a energy
☐ b a ruling
☐ c a dilemma
☐ d an advantage

5 overturn
6 push
7 take up
8 undergo

☐ e the limits
☐ f a ban
☐ g surgery
☐ h running

6 Complete the summary of the article with the correct form of the collocations in exercise 5.

Oscar's parents (1) ____________ when he was born with a congenital disability, but decided to allow him to (2) ____________ to have both lower legs amputated. However, Oscar was undeterred by the amputations and after excelling in a number of other sports at school, he decided to (3) ____________. After achieving remarkable success in paralympic sporting events, he decided to (4) ____________ even further, and compete alongside able-bodied athletes. However, critics complained that his running blades (5) ____________ an unfair ____________ as they allowed him to run at the same speed as non-disabled athletes whilst (6) ____________ less ____________. When he was disqualified from competing in events for able-bodied athletes, Oscar (7) ____________ the ____________, and eventually the IAAF (8) ____________ the ____________.

7 What do you think? Choose the sentence, 1, 2 or 3, that best matches your opinion and say why.

1 Disabled athletes should be allowed to compete in non-disabled events using artificial aids.
2 Disabled athletes should be allowed to compete in non-disabled events, but without using artificial aids.
3 Disabled athletes should not be allowed to compete in non-disabled events.

READ & LISTEN

8 **20** Listen to Reading 10 *Oscar Pistorius: the fastest man on no legs* on the CD and read the article again.

Oscar Pistorius: the fastest man on no legs

1) It was not a promising start for a man who was to become a world champion sprinter and reach the pinnacle of his sport. When Oscar Pistorius was born in Johannesburg, South Africa, in 1986, he was diagnosed with a congenital condition which meant that he had no fibulae (lower leg bones). His parents faced an agonizing dilemma: either he would have to undergo surgery, or he would be confined to a wheelchair for the rest of his life. They opted for surgery, and so at the age of 11 months Oscar had both his lower legs amputated, and learned to walk using prosthetic (artificial) limbs below the knee.

2) Spurred on by ambitious parents who encouraged him to compete regardless of his double amputation, Oscar took up sports at school. He excelled in sporting activities, including rugby union, water polo, tennis and cricket, and won trophies for wrestling and boxing. Later, he took up running as part of a rehabilitation programme for a rugby injury, using specially designed running blades in place of his normal prosthetic limbs. In 2004, he won his first international gold medal at the Athens Paralympic Games, an international sporting competition for people with disabilities, held in the same year as the Olympics. Four years later, he was a triple gold medallist at the Beijing Paralympics in 2008, where he became the first ever Paralympian to win Gold in each of the 100m, 200m and 400m sprints. Since then he has gone on to break his own world sprinting records for disabled athletes over 30 times.

3) Oscar's remarkable sprinting prowess has been made possible by his famous 'Cheetahs', the hyper-engineered 'running feet' that enable him to run at speeds hitherto undreamed of by disabled athletes, and which have earned him the nickname 'The Blade Runner'. Made of super-light carbon fibre, these elegant blades are constantly upgraded by their Icelandic designers to allow their wearer to achieve an ever more streamlined performance. But ironically, it is their very effectiveness which has placed Pistorius at the centre of one of sport's most heated recent controversies.

4) When Pistorius started competing in events alongside able-bodied athletes, and winning his first medals, he faced accusations that his running blades conferred an unfair advantage in comparison with non-disabled rivals. In 2007, a study commissioned by the IAAF (International Association of Athletics Federations) reported that the blades not only added length to his stride, but also allowed him to run at the same speed as able-bodied sprinters whilst expending 25% less energy. Pistorius was disqualified from taking part in events for non-disabled athletes but, having enlisted his own team of lawyers, he contested the ruling, protesting that it was he who was at a disadvantage since he had less blood in his body and no calf muscles. Five months later, the case was dropped on the grounds that the evidence was inconclusive, and the ban was overturned.

5) Undeterred by the legal wrangling surrounding his performance, the hyper-competitive athlete has continued to push the limits in his quest for ever greater personal achievement. As well as qualifying for the London Olympic Games (400m sprint and 4x400 relay), he has also won a number of awards, including the prestigious Laureus World Sports Award for Sportsperson of the Year with a Disability. However, Pistorius insists that he wants to be known not as a disabled athlete, but simply as a sportsperson. Sportsmanship is not just about winning medals, he says; what matters is achieving your personal best.

6) Whatever the future holds in store for Pistorius, one thing is clear: his achievements have taken the world of athletics into uncharted ethical waters, and have challenged us all to rethink the boundaries between able-bodied and disabled sportspeople. To quote Oscar's motto: 'You are not disabled by your disabilities, but abled by your abilities'. His passion and commitment make him not only a role model for disabled sportsmen and sportswomen, but also an inspiration for any aspiring athlete.

11A | A sight for sore eyes

Descriptive verbs

1 Match the verbs in the box to the pictures A–F.

shine	sparkle	toss	flash	float	flutter

A
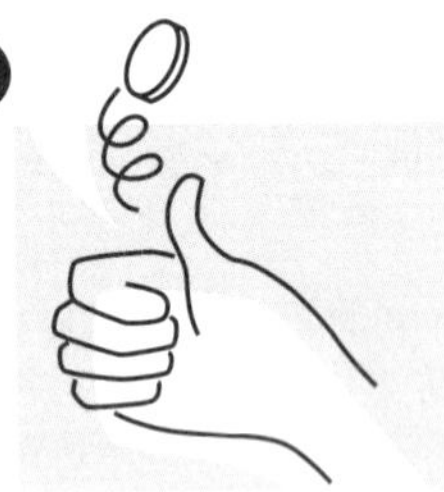

D
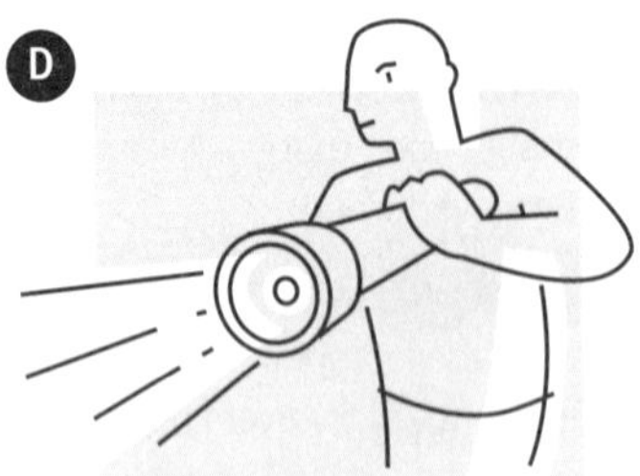

B

E
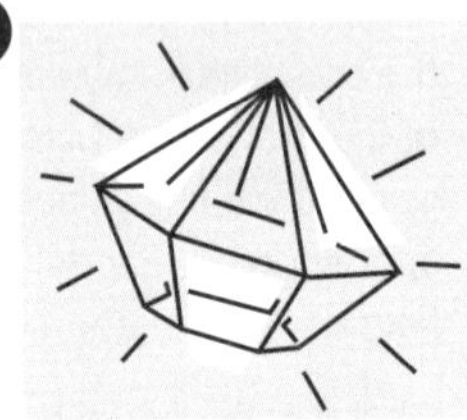

C
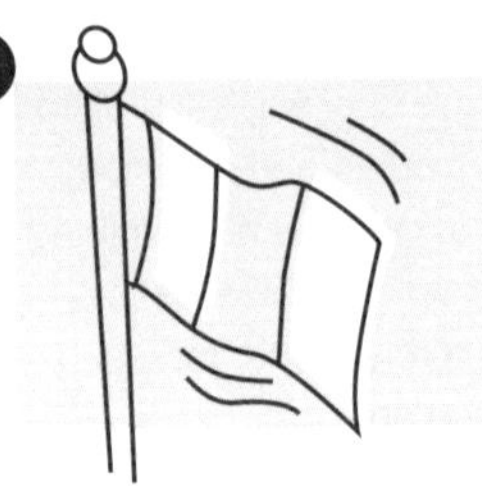

F

2 Write sentences to describe the pictures in exercise 1.

1 ______________________________________.
2 ______________________________________.
3 ______________________________________.
4 ______________________________________.
5 ______________________________________.
6 ______________________________________.

3 Match the sentence beginnings 1–6 in column A to the endings a–f in column B.

A
1 If you're bored in class
2 If you're house-hunting
3 If you have time to spend in a bookshop
4 If you're in a hurry
5 If you're amused
6 If you're fascinated

B
☐ a you glance at something.
☐ b you browse.
☐ c you view properties.
☐ d your eyes twinkle.
☐ e your mind wanders.
☐ f you gaze.

4 Complete the verses with a suitable form of the verbs in the box. Three are not needed.

flutter	glance	stare	toss	twinkle	wander

1 __________, __________ little star
How I wonder what you are
Up above the world so high
Like a diamond in the sky

2 I love to go __________
Along the mountain track
And as I go I laugh and sing
My knapsack on my back

3 Mix a pancake,
Beat a pancake,
Put it in a pan.
Cook a pancake,
__________ a pancake,
Catch it if you can.

Translation

5 Translate the text into your language.

Ring out, wild bells
by Alfred, Lord Tennyson

Ring out, wild bells, to the wild sky,
The flying cloud, the frosty light;
The year is dying in the night;
Ring out, wild bells, and let him die.

Ring out the old, ring in the new,
Ring, happy bells, across the snow:
The year is going, let him go;
Ring out the false, ring in the true.

____
____
____

11B | Affordable art

DETERMINERS, PRONOUNS & QUANTIFIERS

1 Find two correct sentences and correct the incorrect ones.

1 Shall we go to other place?
2 I have all intention of going to the show.
3 My both sisters are lawyers.
4 Neither of them is good at art.
5 I'm staying here for other six weeks.
6 For all my efforts, I failed the exam.

2 Rearrange the words to make sentences and questions.

1 you to money what all are do this going with ?

____

2 for worked time I here quite have some .

____

3 yet any these met people of she has ?

____

4 a quite I few home books got more at have .

____

5 as other well of writes neither as my this pens .

____

6 little cake have this of please I a more could ?

____

3 Underline the expression that refers to a larger quantity.

1 plenty of / enough
2 few / a few
3 little / very little
4 a few / quite a few
5 several / a couple of
6 no / very few

4 Complete the sentences with words or phrases from exercise 3 so that they are true for you.

1 I know __________ about modern art.
2 There are __________ famous paintings in my local gallery.
3 __________ artists are famous in their lifetime.
4 __________ people can afford original art.
5 I have __________ posters up in my room.
6 I have __________ money.

PREPOSITIONAL PHRASES

5 Complete the table with the words in the box.

chance danger display fault fire
leave leisure mistake nature person
retrospect risk stake strike tears

IN	AT
ON	BY

6 Complete the sentences with the phrases from exercise 5. More than one may be possible.

1 Sorry, I didn't mean to delete that file – I did it __________.
2 I came across this article __________ as I was browsing the internet.
3 __________, we should have taken more safety precautions. It was foolish to put people's lives __________.
4 If the manufacturer is found to be __________, you have the right to compensation.
5 The paintings are __________ in the main gallery from next week.

7 Complete the prepositional phrases in the sentences with the correct noun.

1 I'm surprised he reacted like that – it was completely out of __________.
2 People who are out of __________ are entitled to receive unemployment benefits.
3 I'm afraid I'll be off __________ on Friday, but I'll be back at the office next week.
4 I'm so unfit – even running 100 metres leaves me out of __________.
5 You can play anywhere you like except for the library, which I'm afraid is off __________.
6 Don't get your facts from articles that are out of __________.

11c | The sound of silence

Sounds

1 Underline the noun in the groups a–h that does not correspond to the verb 1–8.

1	beep	a	horns, alarm clock, drum
2	click	b	footsteps, camera, fingers
3	creak	c	floorboard, coins, door
4	howl	d	wind, wolf, plane
5	hum	e	fridge, keys, conversation
6	rumble	f	wind, thunder, stomach
7	screech	g	brakes, balloon, tyres
8	sizzle	h	sausages, fly, bacon

2 Match the pictures A–H to the correct sound from the box.

buzz	chime	clatter	clink
jingle	plop	pop	rustle

A
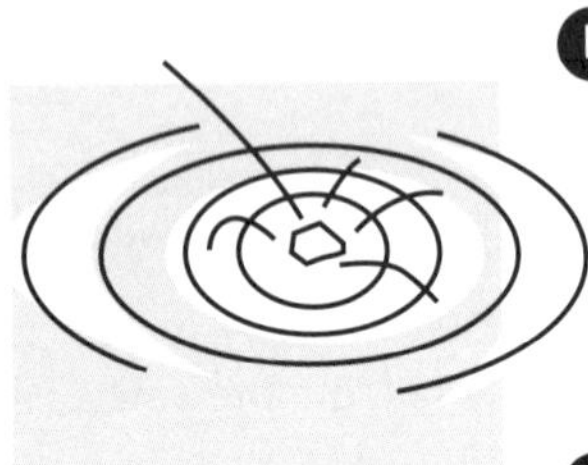

E

B
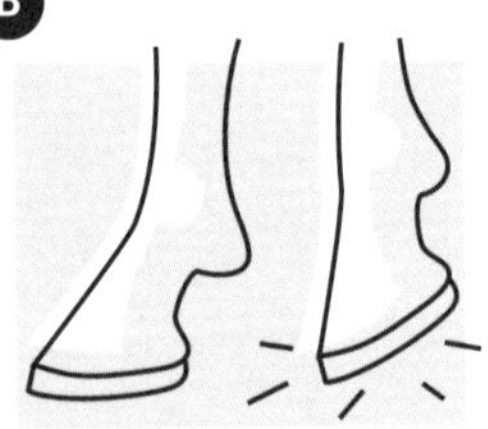

F
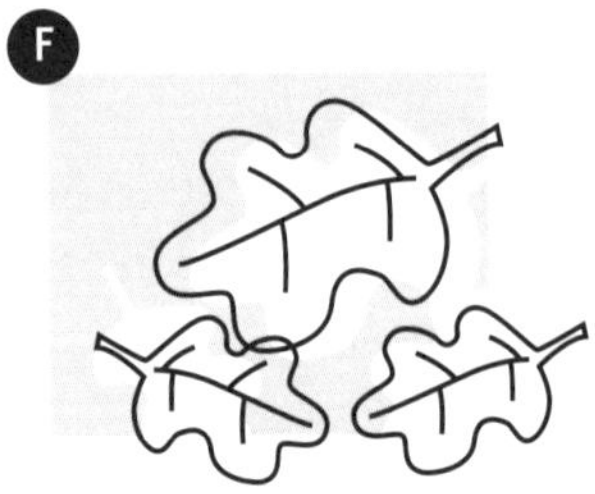

C
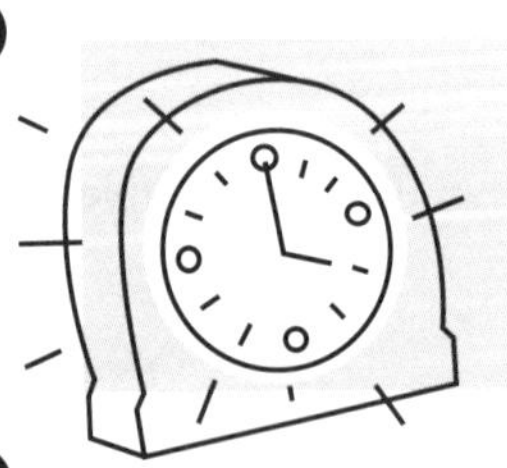

G

D
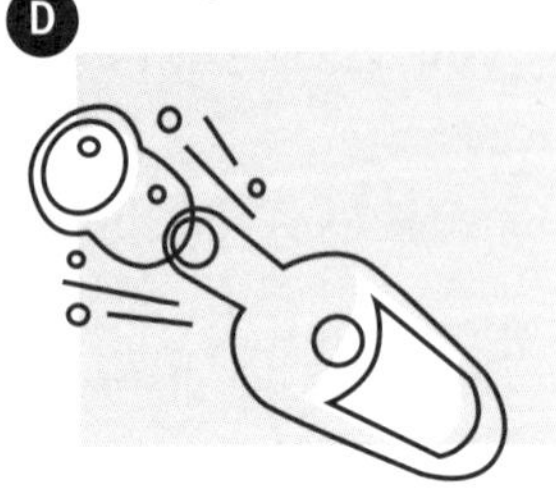

H

Vocabulary from the lesson

3 Match the adjectives 1–6 in column A to the definitions a–f in column B.

A

1	anonymous	4	incongruous
2	dim	5	jagged
3	disconcerting	6	unassuming

B

- ☐ a strange because of being very different to other things which happen or exist in the same situation
- ☐ b a surface or edge that has a lot of rough pointed parts that make it look broken or torn
- ☐ c making you feel worried, confused or surprised
- ☐ d not bright
- ☐ e something that has no interesting or unusual features
- ☐ f behaving in a quiet and pleasant way, without trying to appear better or more important than other people

4 Complete the text with the adjectives from exercise 3.

> I entered the room and looked around. In the (1) __________ light I could just make out a table and two chairs, and an unmade bed in the corner. With no pictures on the wall, and no trinkets, the room looked rather (2) __________, and I wondered who could be living there. Someone rather humble and (3) __________, I imagined. Just then I noticed a teddy bear on the bed, looking strangely (4) __________ in the adult environment. Even more (5) __________ was the (6) __________ glass from a broken window where someone had clearly tried to break into the room.

Dictation

5 **21** Write the text that you hear.

____

____

____

____

____

____

____

11D | The sound of music

Hypothetical present & future situations

1 Underline the best response, a, b or c.

1 'You really should take a break from work.'
a) I wish I would!
b) If only I can!
c) If only I could!

2 'Do you mind if I smoke?'
a) I'd rather not.
b) I'd rather you didn't.
c) I'd rather you don't.

3 'Do you work part-time?'
a) I wish I did!
b) I wish I would!
c) If only I would!

4 'We're playing in the final tomorrow!'
a) I wish you would win!
b) I hope you win!
c) I wish you could win!

5 'Stop it and come here at once!'
a) I wish you wouldn't shout at me!
b) I wish you didn't shout at me!
c) I wish you don't shout at me!

6 'The photocopier's out of order again.'
a) It's high time to get a new one.
b) It's about time they get a new one.
c) It's high time they got a new one.

2 Delete the incorrect alternative.

A

It's time we did the dishes. / It's time to do the dishes.

B

It's time we did the dishes. / It's time to do the dishes.

3 Complete the second sentence so that it means the same as the first.

1 Life would be a lot simpler if we didn't have to commute to work.
Imagine ______________________________.

2 Thanks to you, I've got a good job.
If it ______________________________.

3 I don't have a well-paid job because I didn't go to university.
If ______________________________.

4 Going out would be more fun than staying in.
I'd sooner ______________________________.

5 If he asked me out, I'd say no.
If he were ______________________________.
Were ______________________________.

Dislocation

4 Rearrange the words to form sentences with a noun phrase tag at the end.

1 won that supposing award you it ?
____

2 piece chance it good winning stands a of your .
____

3 think fascinating I your sounds it idea .
____

4 the worked project have pupils hard they on the .
____

5 silence a what idea strange recording !
____

6 forks jingly and they nice knives make sounds .
____

5 Complete the questions using the phrases from the box.

A title	That music competition
That new piece	The competition entry
The concert	The prize money

1 ____________, are you planning to go in for it?
2 ____________, have you submitted it yet?
3 ____________, when are you going to perform it?
4 ____________, have you decided on one?
5 ____________, when will it be put on?
6 ____________, how shall we spend it?

11 | Reading

1 Read the definition of *busker* and match the words and phrases in the box to the pictures A–G.

> **busker** /'bʌskə(r)/ noun [C]
> someone who performs music in the streets and other public places for money

acrobat	fire-eater	juggler	living statue
magician	mime artist	puppeteer	

2 Which statement is true of you, 1, 2 or 3?

1 I rarely or never give money to buskers.
2 I often give money to buskers.
3 I sometimes give money to buskers, depending on the quality of their performance.

3 Read the article about busking. Where do you think it is taken from, 1, 2 or 3?

1 an online encyclopaedia
2 a website for buskers
3 a magazine article

4 Choose the best titles a–h for the paragraphs 1–8 in the article.

☐ a Keep an eye on your earnings.
☐ b Look presentable.
☐ c Entertainment is the name of the game.
☐ d The key to success is playing the right tunes.
☐ e Make sure you're not breaking the law.
☐ f Use your business sense.
☐ g Only do it if you enjoy it.
☐ h Choose where you perform carefully.

5 Find evidence from the article to support these statements.

1 Street performing is becoming more popular internationally.
2 There are many different forms of street entertainment other than busking.
3 Earning money is not the only motivation for busking.
4 Some people may cause problems if you busk in their favourite spot.
5 Audiences are not always appreciative of buskers' performances.
6 You can earn more money by playing people's favourite tunes.
7 Novelty is more important than musical ability.
8 You shouldn't rely on busking to make a living.

6 Find words or phrases in the article which match the definitions 1–8 below.

1 making just enough money to survive ______________
2 fame ______________
3 to steal ______________
4 usual or expected in a particular situation ______________
5 excitement ______________
6 all the songs a performer knows and can perform ______________
7 to increase the money people give ______________
8 the praise or respect you gain through your achievements ______________

READ & LISTEN

7 **22** Listen to Reading 11 *That's entertainment!* on the CD and read the article again.

THAT'S ENTERTAINMENT!

From jugglers to street theatre, puppeteers to human statues, the art of street entertainment is enjoying something of a resurgence in many parts of the world. Perhaps the most familiar street performer is the busker – the lone Lennon-lookalike strumming old Beatles tunes on a guitar on a street corner, the astoundingly-talented string quartet entertaining passers-by in a busy shopping mall, or the down-and-out blowing plaintively into a harmonica in the Underground – but street entertainers come in many shapes and sizes. Magicians, clowns, acrobats, fire-eaters, unicyclists, mime artists, one-man bands, and even snake charmers and sword swallowers all compete for the attention of the passing hordes in the hope that they will toss a coin into their upturned cases and reward their performances.

What is the attraction of busking? For some it's a way of eking out a living, for others it's a means of supplementing meagre earnings, or supporting themselves while they are studying or travelling round the world. But for many people busking has become a way of life they would not wish to change. The word 'busk' comes from the Spanish verb 'buscar' meaning 'to seek', so buskers seek not only monetary appreciation, but also appreciation of their performances. Busking can be a way of sharing your talents with the world, and for a lucky few it can even be a ticket to stardom. Bob Dylan, Kanye West and Jon Bon Jovi, just to mention a few, all started out as buskers before their musical abilities were discovered.

So what should you do if you want to make it as a street performer? We went out onto the streets of the capital and asked buskers for their top tips.

1 ____________________

A good pitch is the secret of success. But competition can be fierce, and some performers can hassle you if you try to muscle in on their pitch. The best place is outside restaurants where you have a captive audience, but other good spots include open-air markets and busy shopping streets. But avoid obstructing people so that they have to go out of their way to avoid you. That annoys people and is counter-productive in terms of earning money. **Aidan, Australia**

2 ____________________

People are less inclined to part with their hard-earned cash if you look as if you've been sleeping rough for the last month. **Javier, Spain**

3 ____________________

In some places you need a permit to busk, and if you're caught without one you may be moved on or even end up in jail in some countries. **Ken, Japan**

4 ____________________

You'll need to look out for people who try to nick coins instead of putting them in. But having said that, people can be incredibly generous too. Yes, some people will chuck in the odd foreign coin, but you get schoolchildren handing you their pocket money and I've even had homeless people tossing in a quid when they go by. It's really heart-warming. **Helle, Denmark**

5 ____________________

Some days you might get a lukewarm response, other days you'll get completely ignored, insulted, laughed at or even sworn at. That's just par for the course, and you shouldn't let it get you down. But nothing can beat the buzz you get when you're playing at the top of your performance and the audience is with you. That's just magic. It makes it all worthwhile. **Gerry, Ireland**

6 ____________________

It's more fun to vary your repertoire, but what tend to get the audience going are the old favourites. You need to be prepared to take requests too. The audience love it if you play 'their song' and it tends to up the contributions as well. **Jon, UK**

7 ____________________

You don't have to be a world-class performer to be a busker, but what you lack in talent you can make up for in originality. People respond to something that's novel. Try to grab the audience's attention with something that is unusual or has a dash of creativity. **Anne-Marie, France**

8 ____________________

You can get decent takings if you set your mind to it. Having CDs on sale gives you some kudos, and sometimes you need to be proactive if business is slow, passing the hat round instead of waiting for people to donate. But, whatever you do, don't give up the day job. Some days you can make over £100, but other days it can be a fraction of that. Busking is fraught with uncertainty and insecurity. **Ben, Romania**

12A | Science fact

Plurals & number

1 Write the plurals of these words.

1 appendix ____________
2 check up ____________
3 daughter-in-law ____________
4 fly ____________
5 goose ____________
6 in-law ____________
7 ox ____________
8 passer-by ____________
9 runner up ____________
10 valley ____________

2 Say whether the words are singular (*S*), plural (*P*) or both (*B*).

1 aircraft ___
2 antenna ___
3 cacti ___
4 crisis ___
5 criteria ___
6 deer ___
7 emphases ___
8 formula ___
9 media ___
10 offspring ___
11 phenomena ___
12 sheep ___
13 species ___
14 stimulus ___

3 Complete the table with the words in the box, according to their ending. Some words can go in more than one box.

half memo potato studio wolf
hero mosquito roof thief zoo
loaf photo shelf volcano

1 *-os*	3 *-fs*
2 *-oes*	4 *-ves*

4 Delete the incorrect alternatives (sometimes both a plural and a singular form may be possible).

1 I love *that* / *those* jeans – where did you get *it* / *them*?
2 The audience *was* / *were* in tears at the end of the play.
3 I think physics *is* / *are* fun but maths *is* / *are* boring.
4 The government *is* / *are* setting up a scheme to ensure the unemployed *has* / *have* enough work opportunities.
5 Measles *is* / *are* highly infectious, and people with the illness *is* / *are* advised to stay at home.
6 His earnings *is* / *are* €50 a week, which *isn't* / *aren't* enough to feed a family of ten.
7 The police *has* / *have* asked the public to make sure all personal belongings *is* / *are* removed while the premises *is* / *are* searched.
8 The press *has* / *have* a responsibility to ensure that news *is* / *are* reported accurately.

Vocabulary from the lesson

5 Match the verbs 1–6 in column A to their definitions a–f in column B.

A
1 crack
2 refract
3 replenish
4 scald
5 scatter
6 tickle

B
☐ a to move your fingers gently on someone's skin in order to give them a pleasant feeling or to make them laugh
☐ b to throw or drop things so that they spread over an area
☐ c to burn your skin with very hot liquid or steam
☐ d light travelling in a slightly different direction after it hits a surface such as water or glass, so that the surface appears to bend it
☐ e to make something full again, or to bring it back to its previous level by replacing what has been used
☐ f to make a whip make a short sudden loud noise

12B | Science fiction

VOCABULARY FROM THE LESSON

1 Complete the sentences with the correct form of a word from the box.

bruise	cinder	clasp	close	cripple
dead	leak	let	mumble	rusty

1 After the fall, the racehorse was ___________ and unable to run in any more races.
2 I promised him that I would do my best, and so I don't want to ___________ him down.
3 The hot ___________ falling from the fire burnt a hole in the carpet.
4 I carried the sleeping child like a ___________ weight in my arms.
5 He held out his hand and ___________ my hand tightly.
6 It was a ___________ run thing, but Henderson was elected as President by a narrow majority.
7 The authorities have warned of the potential dangers if the nuclear power station were to develop a ___________.
8 It's not surprising that your tools have become ___________, if you leave them outside in the rain.
9 You're lucky to have survived the accident with no bones broken; but we'd better check that there is no internal ___________.
10 When giving a speech, you should speak naturally, and at a reasonable speed and volume; and make sure you do not ___________.

2 Rearrange the upper case letters to make words.

1 COYUNABY ___________
2 HUMBAS ___________
3 CAKEGREW ___________
4 CLUELOME ___________
5 ATIRANOID ___________
6 DURGOTRACE ___________

3 Match the words 1–6 in exercise 2 to the definitions a–f.

☐ a an attack from a hidden position
☐ b the parts of a vehicle or building that remain after it has been seriously damaged
☐ c the quality of being able to float
☐ d a form of energy produced during a nuclear reaction that is used for making electrical power, but can also kill or harm humans who receive too much of it
☐ e the smallest part of an element or compound that is capable of independent existence
☐ f (of materials) shaped into parallel folds

4 Complete the sentences with *let alone* in a suitable way.

1 The test was so complicated that it was too difficult for the teachers to understand, let alone ___________.
2 She has never travelled outside her own town, let alone ___________.
3 Many people find it difficult to remember what they did last week, let alone ___________.
4 Miss Dalrymple found Mr Lacy so unpleasant that she did not want even to spend time with him, let alone ___________.
5 After spending the whole day fishing we hadn't even seen a fish, let alone ___________.

DICTATION

5 **23** Write the text that you hear.

12c | Sport technology

Verb affixes

1 Find and correct the incorrect word in each group using the appropriate affix *-en*, *-ify*, *-ize* or *-ate*.

1 assassinate, differentiate, dominate, intensificate

____

2 captify, clarify, exemplify, justify

____

3 flatten, heighten, longen, shorten

____

4 categorize, magnifize, maximize, stabilize

____

5 endanger, enrage, enstandard, ensure

____

6 deepen, largen, threaten, widen

____

2 Underline the correct explanation, a or b, for each sentence.

1 He downplayed the importance of the team's defeat.
a) He said it was more important than it was.
b) He said it was less important than it was.

2 We were outnumbered by the other team.
a) The other team had more players.
b) The other team scored more goals.

3 The benefits of sport outweigh the disadvantages.
a) There are more disadvantages than benefits.
b) There are more benefits than disadvantages.

4 We were overcharged at the football match.
a) We paid too much.
b) We exhausted ourselves.

5 They undercut our offer by 20%.
a) They wanted us to pay less.
b) They offered to pay less than us.

6 Sports facilities in this town are underfunded.
a) People should pay more to use them.
b) The authorities should contribute more to their cost.

Vocabulary from the lesson

3 Complete the text with the phrases a–g.

Thank you for your interesting presentation, but I'd just like to pick up (1) ________. You mentioned (2) ________. The main argument (3) ________. However, a strong argument (4) ________. Let's take, (5) ________. On an average cycle it consumes 20 litres of water per wash. And secondly, (6) ________, this is around 3.5kWh per wash. And let's also go back (7) ________ ...

a against their use is the fact that they use up a lot of water and energy
b the advantages of household appliances such as dishwashers
c regarding energy
d to what you said about washing machines
e on what you said about technology in the home
f in favour of these is that they are immensely time-saving and labour-saving
g the dishwasher, for example

Translation

4 Translate the text into your language.

These days, every aspect of sport is influenced by science. This influence can be seen not only in the training schedules and diets of athletes, but also in the clothes they wear and the equipment they use. Teams of scientists are constantly striving to create performance-enhancing footwear and swimsuits that enable swimmers to improve their speeds by fractions of a second. Nowhere is the impact of technology more visible than in the Olympic Games, where electronic tagging and the use of earphones, microphones and high speed cameras has become an important feature of many events. Even Olympic running tracks and sports stadiums are now designed using state-of-the-art technology to maximize competitors' performance.

However, our increasing reliance on technology also confronts us with dilemmas. Some argue that we risk losing the physical challenge that is central to sporting competition. There is also a danger that scientists will be able to develop genetically-enhanced therapies and other drugs that cannot be detected in athletes. And finally, there is the question of whether competitors from poor countries are at a disadvantage in comparison with high-spending teams from the developed world.

12D The end?

1 Choose the correct alternative, a, b or c, to complete the sentences. Each sentence refers to one lesson from the book.

1 I'd like to __ some money, please.
a) transfer b) transform c) convert

2 I __ these tenses at least ten times.
a) have been studying b) have studied c) study

3 These exercises are harder than __ we studied last week.
a) them b) that c) the ones

4 I don't doubt the __ of his answer.
a) sincereness b) sincerecy c) sincerity

5 We'd better not __ any longer.
a) wait b) to wait c) waiting

6 Start by __ seven cards to each player.
a) drawing b) dealing c) shuffling

7 He always __ out of his way to help.
a) gets b) gives c) goes

8 My bike is __ near as nice as yours.
a) nowhere b) nothing c) hardly

9 I'm afraid I'm __ of money at the moment.
a) lacking b) short c) shortage

10 Strange __ it may seem, I really enjoy tests.
a) as b) but c) however

11 He drove at a speed __ excess of 100kph.
a) at b) in c) to

12 What happened was __ my keys.
a) that I lost b) to lose c) lose

13 She was lying through her __.
a) mouth b) teeth c) lips

14 He suggested __ my job.
a) me to change b) me changing c) I change

15 You __ the life out of me!
a) frightened b) shocked c) surprised

16 Even though he felt self-conscious, he __ a speech.
a) could make b) managed making c) was able to make

17 I have four brothers, two __ are doctors.
a) of whom b) whom c) who

18 Let's go, __?
a) will we b) shall we c) do we

19 The jobs market is __ competitive.
a) highly b) strongly c) deeply

20 If I __ more when I was at university, I might have a better job now.
a) would have studied b) had studied c) would study

21 We urgently need vaccines to deal with the cholera __.
a) outbreak b) outset c) breakout

22 The patient __ in hospital.
a) is treating b) is being treated c) is been treated

23 He should __ greater care with his spelling.
a) pay b) take c) give

24 My watch is broken – I need __.
a) to get it fixed b) to have fixed it c) fixing it

25 Is he at a __ school or a single sex one?
a) comprehensive b) mixed c) dual sex

26 Please be __ your best behaviour.
a) on b) at c) in

27 __ the news, she burst into tears.
a) Having heard b) Hearing c) Heard

28 He was convicted __ assault.
a) for b) of c) with

29 The new traffic scheme is good for __.
a) car owners b) car's owners c) cars' owners

30 She has a(n) __ to lose her temper.
a) attitude b) streak c) tendency

31 Shakespeare is __ Britain's greatest playwright.
a) surely b) understandably c) undoubtedly

32 Don't shout at him for getting it wrong – __, it is his first day at work.
a) admittedly b) mind you c) after all

33 What time __ we meet tonight?
a) will b) shall c) would

34 I'm afraid the house is in poor __.
a) condition b) state c) situation

35 Rarely __ such an excellent book.
a) have I read b) I have read c) I read

36 Two cars were involved in a(n) __ collision.
a) oncoming b) incoming c) head-on

37 Well done! All your hard work has __.
a) worked out b) turned out c) paid off

38 He's on the point __ the race.
a) of winning b) that he'll win c) to win

39 The heavens opened and there was a torrential __.
a) heatwave b) thunderbolt c) downpour

40 You __ smoke in a no-smoking area.
a) don't have to b) mustn't c) needn't

41 I'm afraid I only had a quick __ at the text.
a) browse b) gaze c) glance

42 I'll be here __ weeks.
a) another four b) other four c) four other

43 We heard the __ of champagne corks.
a) plopping b) clinking c) popping

44 I wish you __ humming that song!
a) stopped b) would stop c) were to stop

45 What are your __ for success?
a) criteriae b) criteria c) criterias

46 I can't afford a new bicycle, let __ a car.
a) down b) alone c) for

47 The government is trying to __ the region.
a) stabilify b) enstable c) stabilize

48 It's a pity the course has __ to an end.
a) reached b) arrived c) come

12 | Reading

1 Read the article and answer the questions, a, bor c.

1 Where do you think the text was taken from?
a) A newspaper report
b) An advertisement for space flights
c) A scientific journal

2 Where does the spacecraft travel?
a) to the edge of the Earth's atmosphere
b) into space
c) to the Moon

2 Put these events in the correct order. The first one has been done for you.

- [ ] watch the sky change colour
- [ ] experience weightlessness
- [1] take part in pre-flight preparation
- [ ] take precautions to adjust to the change in speed
- [ ] admire the view of the Earth
- [ ] receive your wings
- [ ] prepare mentally for the next stage
- [ ] experience a sudden silence

3 Choose the correct answer, a, b or c, to complete the sentences.

1 The aim of Virgin Galactic is
a) to make it possible for anyone to afford space travel.
b) to make space travel safer.
c) to make space travel simpler and more widely-available.

2 The journey beyond the atmosphere takes place
a) in the mother ship.
b) in a separate spacecraft.
c) in the mother ship and spacecraft together.

3 During the final phase of the journey
a) the spacecraft changes to adapt to conditions.
b) the power of the spacecraft engine increases.
c) the spacecraft travels more quickly.

4 Underline the false claims in the advertisement.

Take the trip of a lifetime!

1 Enjoy unimaginable experiences.
2 Travel faster than the speed of light.
3 Admire views of the Earth as you have never seen them before.
4 Float around in the spacecraft in zero gravity.
5 Witness the Aurora Borealis.
6 Get to know your fellow astronauts and crew before the trip.
7 Take home a special souvenir of the trip.
8 No training needed.

5 Choose the best explanation of the words and phrases as used in the article, a or b.

1 exhaustive
a) very tiring
b) thorough

2 instantly
a) immediately
b) for a short time

3 hurtle
a) move slowly
b) move quickly

4 hush
a) sense of shock
b) a sudden silence

5 on a high
a) far above the Earth
b) feeling happy and excited

6 spellbound
a) worried
b) impressed and lost in thought

7 glide
a) smooth, noiseless movement
b) slow, irregular movement

6 What do you think? Choose the sentence, 1, 2 or 3, that best matches your opinion and say why.

1 I would love to go on a trip like this.
2 I would never go on a trip like this.
3 I might contemplate going on a trip like this one day.

Read & listen

7 **24** Listen to Reading 12 *Space trek* on the CD and read the article again.

SPACE TREK

Virgin Galactic's goal is to end the exclusivity attached to manned space travel, which means that almost anyone can fly to space safely without the need for special expertise or exhaustive, time-consuming training. The journey starts from the moment you make a firm reservation and book your place amongst the first to go. There will be three days of pre-flight preparation, bonding and training onsite at the spaceport. In the lead-up to your flight, we will keep you fully involved and informed, and there will be opportunities to contribute ideas and participate in pre-flight events.

Astronauts tell us that nothing can really prepare you for your first experience of space, but we will ensure that you are fully-equipped to savour every second of an experience which will be intense and truly unforgettable. And your comfort and enjoyment will be our primary aim right up until you leave the spaceport, complete with a fully-documented record of the whole experience and of course, with your astronaut wings!

Are You Ready?

Your journey to space will be one of incredible contrast and sensory overload. From the spaceport to 50,000ft, you will be in the spacecraft attached to the mother ship, a specially-designed jet carrier aircraft. It will be a time of anticipation and perhaps contemplation of what lies ahead. You will already have met the rest of your crew and you will enjoy the confidence that has come from preparing with them and the pilots for the trip you are about to take together.

Then the countdown to release, a brief moment of quiet before a wave of unimaginable power surges through the craft. You are instantly pinned back into your seat, enthralled by the howl of the rocket motor and the eye-watering acceleration which, as you watch the read-out, has you travelling, in a matter of seconds, at almost 2,500mph – over three times the speed of sound. As you hurtle through the edges of the atmosphere, you watch through the large windows as the cobalt blue sky slowly turns to mauve and indigo and finally to black. You're on a high – this is really happening, you're loving it and you're coping well. You start to relax; but in an instant your senses are back on full alert. The world contained in your spaceship has been completely transformed.

The rocket motor has been switched off and there is a deep hush. The silence of space is as awe-inspiring as was the noise of the rocket just moments earlier. But what is overwhelming your senses now is that the gravity which has dominated your every movement since the day you were born has disappeared.

There is no up and no down and you're out of your seat, experiencing the freedom that you never imagined, even in your wildest dreams. After a graceful mid-space somersault you find yourself staring out of a large window and what you see would make your hair stand on end if the zero gravity hadn't already achieved that effect. Below you (or is it above you?) is a view that you've seen in countless images. But the reality is so much more beautiful, so much more vivid and you are flooded with intense but indefinable emotions. The blue map, curving into the black distance, is familiar, but with none of the usual marked boundaries. The incredibly narrow ribbon of atmosphere looks worryingly fragile. What you are looking at is the source of everything it means to be human, and it is home. You see that your fellow astronauts are equally spellbound, all lost in their own thoughts and storing away the memories.

Then the pilots are asking you to return to your now reclined seats. Gravity is starting to return as you knew it had to. The deceleration produces strong G forces*, but you're lying down and deal with them just as you've been taught. You can hear and feel the feathered wings of the spacecraft producing a powerful drag as the thickness of the atmosphere increases, although out of the windows it still looks like space. The G forces quickly ease off and you hear the pilot announce that she is about to re-feather the craft for the graceful glide home.

Later that evening, after the celebrations and wings ceremony, you are finally alone and know that life will never quite be the same again. You also know you need to sleep, although maybe there is just time to dream about a trip through the Aurora Borealis … now that really would be something.

*sensations caused by changes in speed or direction

Writing for Advanced students

At Advanced level, writing is an area which presents continuing challenges and opportunities for improvement. You may need to improve your writing for work, study or general communication, or to take examinations. At this level, you should feel comfortable writing a wide range of text types, and you should be aware of the structure and conventions that each one demands. You should also pay particular attention to writing accurately, to extending the range of structures, vocabulary and expressions that you use, and to writing in an appropriate register.

In order to improve your writing at this level, here are a few helpful hints.

- Read as widely as possible, for pleasure as well as for work and study. That way you will start to get a feel for natural and idiomatic use of language in different genres.
- Make a note of key vocabulary, expressions, collocations and sentence structures in books or articles that you read. Be particularly aware of developing a range of synonyms and near synonyms, noting differences in usage. Record these in a vocabulary notebook (organized in different sections) and make an effort to reproduce them in your writing.
- Be aware of the mistakes you often make, by paying attention to corrections and feedback from your teachers and fellow students. When you receive your work back, copy it out again. Before you submit a piece of work, check it for errors of grammar, spelling and punctuation. That way you will develop the habit of monitoring your writing for inaccuracies.
- Experiment with different ways of generating ideas for your writing. Discuss with other people how they plan their writing, and try out different ways (eg brainstorming ideas on paper, making a mind map) in order to find out what works best for you.
- Remember that a good piece of writing is rarely finished after the first draft. When you have finished it, leave it for a day or two and return to it to try to make it better. If possible, exchange your work with another person and give each other advice on how it could be improved. This may involve cutting, rewriting, expanding or changing the order of ideas.
- With essays, narratives and letters, pay attention to paragraph structure. Your paragraphs should not be too short or too long. Plan each paragraph and make sure that each one has a clear first sentence that contains the key idea, and that the rest of the paragraph supports that idea.
- When writing and revising your work, try to use a wide range of vocabulary, expressions and structure. You may find it helpful to refer to the *Macmillan English Dictionary for Advanced Learners* which has 'Improve your writing skills' and 'Expand your vocabulary' sections. However, do not force too many difficult words or obscure expressions into your writing, as that may make it seem unnatural.
- Finally, develop the habit of writing for pleasure – letters to friends, noting your ideas and impressions about studying, writing a diary in English, or even trying to write creatively in English. That way your writing may seem less like a chore and more like a pleasure.

Workbook writing lessons

There are six writing units in the Workbook. Each unit consists of two pages (A & B) which practise and build on the writing lessons in the Student's Book.

Page A provides **additional practice of the language focus points** presented in the Student's Book. Use these pages alongside the Student's Book writing lessons.

Page B provides **a structured writing 'lesson', building up to a writing task**. These pages tie in with the topics of the even numbered units in the Student's Book. Sample answers for these writing tasks are provided in the answer key (pages xiii–xvi).

Student's Book		Workbook
Unit 1	An autobiography	1A An autobiography
Unit 2		1B A biography
Unit 3	An article	2A A website article
Unit 4		2B A blog
Unit 5	A work email	3A A work email
Unit 6		3B An email to a friend
Unit 7	A narrative	4A A narrative
Unit 8		4B A description
Unit 9	A letter of complaint	5A A letter of complaint
Unit 10		5B A letter of thanks
Unit 11	An essay	6A An essay (1)
Unit 12		6B An essay (2)

Useful language to improve your writing

Writing about the past

In retrospect, ...
Looking back, ...
I remember X as ...
X marked a major turning point for me
X was the highlight of (my schooldays, my trip, etc)
To cut a long story short ...

Giving advice

Make a point of ...-*ing*
Consider ...-*ing*
Try to ...
Make time to ...
Make sure you ...
Most importantly, learn how to ...

Sending an attachment

Here's (a copy of) ...
I am sending/forwarding with this email ...
Attached is/are ...
I attach ...
Please find attached ...

Introducing key events in a story

Just then, ...
All of a sudden, ...
It was at that moment that ...
Just as he was leaving, ...

Listing problems

The first and most serious problem is ...
A further problem is ...
I am also concerned about ...
In addition, ...
Finally, ...

Writing a conclusion

In conclusion, ...
To conclude, ...
To sum up, ...
On balance, ...
In short, ...

Writing a letter of thanks

I am writing to express my gratitude for ...
This is just to say a big thank you for ...
I am writing to extend our sincere thanks for ...

Writing a letter

I am writing on behalf of/in response to ...
Just a brief note to say ...
I am interested in applying for the position of X.
I look forward to hearing from you.

Time phrases

From that time onwards ...
From then on ...
Not long after that ...
Soon afterwards ...
During the next ten years ...
During this period ...
Around this time ...

Making a deduction

If so, then you may well ...
If the answer is yes, you could ...
If not, then you are likely ...
If the answer is no, then you should certainly ...
If you can't, the chances are that ...

Expressing a viewpoint

It is widely believed that ...
All the evidence suggests that ...
I would argue that ...
It is often claimed that ...
There can be no doubt that ...
It is my view that ...

Recounting an experience

To make matters worse ...
Imagine my embarrassment when ...
Anyway, ...
At this point ...
The moral of the story is ...

1A | WRITING An autobiography

LANGUAGE FOCUS

Time expressions

1 Complete the text with the time expressions in the box.

some day	at the age of five	currently
three years later	ever since	in two years' time
as a child	to date	for the last few months

DRAMA QUEEN

Hi! My name's Julia. I'm (1) __________ in my first year at drama school, and I'll be graduating (2) __________. I was bitten by the acting bug a long time ago. I went to see my first film (3) __________ and I've dreamed of being an actress (4) __________. (5) __________ I used to enjoy dressing up and acting in front of my family and friends, and I had a small part in my first play in my first year at secondary school. Then, (6) __________ I played the part of Eliza Doolittle in the school production of *My Fair Lady*. After I left school, I applied for a place at drama school and I was thrilled when I was offered a place. (7) __________ I've been trying to make contacts in the film industry and I've had walk-on parts in four films (8) __________. I'm hoping that (9) __________ I'll get my big break and get a leading role in a major production. Oh well – you can dream!

Describing your family

2 Complete the second sentence so that it means the same as the first.

1 Ben is the son of my mother and my stepfather.
Ben is my ______________________________.

2 I have two brothers and one sister.
I have three ______________________________.

3 I have two parents and one brother.
There are four ______________________________.

4 My sister Maria is older than me.
Maria is my ______________________________.

5 My grandparents took care of me as a child.
I was ______________________________.

6 As a child I was very happy.
I had ______________________________.

7 My family all get on well and do a lot together.
We are a ______________________________.

8 I have no brothers or sisters.
I am ______________________________.

9 My parents imposed lots of rules and discipline.
I had a ______________________________.

Verb-noun collocations

3 Correct eight mistakes with verb-noun collocations in the letter.

Dear Mr Greig,

I am writing to make application for a scholarship to do a training as a solicitor in your law firm. As you will see from the enclosed CV, I did my secondary school in London, and after graduating from school seven years ago, I made a gap year, during which time I did a placement in the law firm Marks and Melson in Edinburgh.

I then achieved a place at Edinburgh University to read law, and gained my degree three years later.
On graduating, I continued at Edinburgh University where I took the Legal Practice Course and made research into international commercial law. I hope to go into the field of patent law after I have been received as a solicitor.

I look forward to hearing from you.

Yours sincerely,

Tom Buchanan

1B | WRITING A biography

READING

1 Read the biography of Susan Anthony and put the paragraphs in the correct order.

☐ Having completed her education in her father's school and at boarding school, she spent fifteen years working as the headmistress of a female academy. In 1849 she made her first public speech against alcohol abuse, and soon afterwards became involved in the temperance and anti-slavery movements, (1) ________________. (2) ________________, she nonetheless possessed a keen mind and ability to inspire.

☐ From then on she became a tireless campaigner for women's rights, touring the country and addressing meetings, until her death in 1906. She was not to live to see the fulfillment of her ambition to secure the vote for women. However, in 1979 her image was chosen for the dollar coin, making her the first woman to be depicted on US currency.

☐ Susan B Anthony, (3) ________________, was born in Adams, Massachusetts, on 15th February 1820. The daughter of Daniel Anthony, (4) ________________, she developed early on in her life a sense of justice and moral purpose that was to inspire her later life.

☐ It was around this time that she met Elizabeth Cady Stanton, (5) ________________, who was to become a life-long friend. In 1869, along with Stanton, she established the National Women's Suffrage Association (NWSA), and three years later she was arrested for violating the voting laws by leading a group of women to the polls to test their right to vote. She became president of the NWSA in 1892, (6) ________________.

2 Which of these movements did Susan Anthony campaign for?

1 Anti-slavery
2 Combating alcohol abuse
3 Racial equality
4 Votes for women

LANGUAGE FOCUS

Phrases in apposition

1 Complete the gaps 1–6 in the biography with the phrases a–f.

a a liberal Quaker and campaigner against the slave trade
b a post she was to hold for the next eight years
c a fellow activist in the crusade for women's suffrage and equal pay
d issues that she would continue to campaign for in the ensuing decade
e one of America's first female civil rights activists
f Shy and compassionate by nature

Future in the past

2 Underline four more examples of future in the past in the biography, including the phrases in exercise 1.

She met Elizabeth Cady Stanton, … who was to become a life-long friend.

Time phrases

3 Find phrases in the biography with a similar meaning to the ones below.

1 from that time onwards
2 not long after that
3 during the next ten years
4 up to the end of her life
5 during this period
6 in her childhood
7 in 1872

WRITING

1 Choose someone who has made a change to the history of your country, eg a campaigner, explorer, activist, thinker, or political or military leader. You could use the internet for your research.

2 Write a biography following this outline:

Paragraph 1: Say why he/she is famous. Give details of his/her birth, family, upbringing and education.
Paragraphs 2–3: Give details of his/her life, including achievements, significant events and character.
Paragraph 4: Describe the period up to his/her death and how he/she will be remembered.

2A | WRITING A website article

LANGUAGE FOCUS

Writing definitions

1 Use your English dictionary to complete the definitions.

1 A workaholic can be defined as someone who ________ ________________________________.
2 An optician is a person who ________________ ________________________________.
3 A financial advisor ________________________ ________________________________.
4 An osteopath ______________________________ ________________________________.
5 A counsellor ______________________________ ________________________________.
6 A dietician _______________________________ ________________________________.

2 Complete the sentences with the words from the box.

urge	addicted	withdrawal	obsessed
live	craving	compulsion	dependent

1 Maxine is __________ on her mobile phone.
2 Matt can't __________ without his mp3 player.
3 Fay can't resist the __________ to buy the latest fashion.
4 Tania suffers from __________ symptoms if she can't watch her favourite TV show.
5 Wendy is __________ to her daily workout.
6 Chris is __________ with crosswords.
7 Tracy suffers from a __________ to text her friends.
8 Penny has a __________ for pizzas.

Making a deduction

3 Match the first sentences 1–6 in column A to the second sentences a–f in column B.

A

1 Are you putting on weight and feeling unfit?
2 Do you find it easy to relax when you aren't working?
3 Do you frequently suffer from backache?
4 Are you feeling anxious and stressed?
5 Are you careful with your money and never run up debts?
6 Can you read small print without difficulty?

B

☐ a If so, then you may well find it helpful to see a counsellor.
☐ b If the answer is yes, you could consider seeing a dietician.
☐ c If not, then you are likely to benefit from a consultation with a financial advisor.
☐ d If the answer is no, then you should certainly make an appointment to see an optician.
☐ e If you do, then you may need to see an osteopath.
☐ f If you don't, the chances are that you are a workaholic.

Describing cause & effect

4 Rearrange the words to make sentences.

1 disease in factor is heart risk a smoking .
____
2 sunstroke in result excessive can sunbathing .
____
3 front too can in strain long in a result eye sitting of computer .
____
4 due often is overwork tiredness to .
____
5 is infection of poor cause the hygiene underlying .
____
6 root the violence at boredom of often teenage is .
____
7 temperature of include flu and headaches a symptoms .
____

2B | WRITING A blog

READING

1 Read the blog written for the website 'Your most embarrassing moments'. What were the three things Darren did wrong?

File Edit View Favourites Tools Help Link

Embarrassing moments, eh? Well, I reckon we've all had a few! But the one that springs to mind was the time I'd agreed to give a speech at my best friend's wedding. I'd spent ages thinking up what to say and I'd managed to write three or four pages full of embarrassing stories about the things we'd got up to at college. (1) ______________, there I was waiting for my turn when I suddenly realized that I'd left my notes at home. (2) ______________! I went into a total panic, and just grabbed a paper serviette and jotted down what I could remember. Then I had to walk up to the front clutching my serviette and feeling like a complete idiot. (3) ______________ it all seemed to go OK, and I managed to bluff my way through until I got to the point where I had to propose a toast to the bride and groom, and said 'Let's raise our glasses and wish Ben and Sophie a long and happy life together'. There were several seconds of embarrassed silence before (4) ______________ that I'd said 'Sophie' instead of 'Rachel' – Sophie being Ben's ex-girlfriend, not his wife. So, in an attempt to get myself out of the hole I'd just dug, I had to go and (5) ______________ by saying, 'Well, let's hope Rachel has better luck than Sophie!' (6) ______________ I just wanted the ground to open and swallow me up. (7) ______________ how mortified I was to get a round of applause and cheers from almost everyone there! It's just as well Ben has a good sense of humour and wasn't too upset about it. Well, there you have it. And (8) ______________? Never agree to give a speech at a wedding!

Darren

2 Decide if the following statements are true (T) or false (F). Underline evidence from the blog to support your answers.

1 Darren was at college with Ben. _____
2 Darren made notes on a paper serviette. _____
3 Ben was getting married to Sophie. _____
4 Darren fell into a hole in the ground. _____
5 Most of the audience enjoyed Darren's speech. _____
6 Ben was angry about the speech. _____

LANGUAGE FOCUS

Narrative expressions

1 Complete the blog in Reading exercise 1 with the words and phrases in the box.

make matters worse	imagine	I suddenly realized
luckily	the moral of the story	anyway
what a nightmare	at this point	

Explaining consequences in the past

2 Complete the sentences about the story.

1 Darren went into a total panic because ______________________________.
2 He felt like a complete idiot because ______________________________.
3 There were several seconds of embarrassed silence because ______________________________.
4 He wanted the ground to open and swallow him up because ______________________________.

WRITING

1 Write a blog describing an embarrassing moment based on the picture below or on a personal experience. Add your own ideas.

Follow this format:
1 Introduce your entry.
2 Set the scene: What had you done before the event? What were you doing when it happened?
3 What happened and how did you feel?
4 What is the moral of the story?

3A | WRITING A work email

LANGUAGE FOCUS

Formal & informal style

1 Complete the expressions used at the end of emails.

Formal

1 Y______ s______
2 Y______ f______

Informal

3 L______ of l______
4 C______!

Neutral

5 K______ r______
6 Y______
7 A______ the b______
8 B______ w______

Making arrangements

2 Put the emails in the correct order.

☐ Re Tues, something has come up. Could we make it Weds eve instead? *Sorry about this.*
A

☐ *Sounds good.* It will be nice to catch up!
P

☐ *How about Friday at 7pm?*
Anna

☐ Peter
Can you make dinner on Tues 10th? We could go to La Capannina. It would be great to see you.
Anna

☐ Friday at 7 at La Capannina will be fine.
See you then
P

☐ *Sorry, I'm tied up on Weds. Could we make it another day?*
P

3 Rewrite the sentences in italics from exercise 2 in a more formal style.

1 I'm sorry to ______________________.
2 Thanks for ______________________.
I'd be ______________________.
3 Would Friday ______________________?
4 Would you be ______________________?
5 I look ______________________.
6 Unfortunately, ______________________.
Could we possibly ______________________?

Making requests

4 Complete the emails with the phrases from the box. More than one answer may be possible.

could you   let me know   you could   please   can you

1 Dear Ms Jones,
__________ send me details of this year's HEA conference?
Many thanks,
Mary Ann Robertson

2 Dear Mary Ann,
I am attaching details of the conference as requested. __________ get back to me ASAP if you would like to attend as the places are filling very fast.
Hilary Jones

3 Dear Mary Ann,
Re your booking for the HEA conference, please __________ if you would like accommodation at the conference centre.
Hilary

4 Dear Hilary,
__________ possibly reserve a single ensuite room for me on Friday and Saturday nights?
Many thanks,
Mary Ann

5 Ed - The keynote speaker for the conference (Chris Travis) will be arriving at 3pm on Friday. Do you think __________ pick him up from the station and give him a lift to the conference centre?
All the best,
Hilary

5 Write a request after these statements.

1 I'm afraid I can't find your CV. Do you think you could ______________________?
2 I need to talk to you urgently. Can you ______________________?
3 I'm interested in applying for the post of librarian. Could you possibly ______________________?
4 Charles's leaving party is on Friday at Hania's house. Please let me know ______________________.
5 The meeting starts at 9am. Please ______________________.
6 I can pick you up from the airport if you like. Let me know ______________________.

3B | WRITING An email to a friend

READING

1 Read the email exchange and answer the questions.

1 Are Liz and Sonia recent friends, old friends or colleagues?
2 What do they decide to do together?
3 Where and when will they meet?
4 What news does each give?

Dear Liz,

It feels like a long time since we were in touch. I hope you are well and life is good for you. I'm well, busy as ever. Josh is about to start school in September – how time flies! I'm just dropping you a line because I've joined a fitness club (Energize) and we get free guest passes for the first month. How do you fancy coming along as my guest and trying out the facilities? There's an amazing pool with a sauna, steam room and jacuzzi, as well as a state-of-the-art gym. There's also a nice restaurant where we could have lunch. Let me know if you'd like to come – Saturday 16th would be best for me as Josh is staying with my parents that weekend, but failing that I could manage 23rd. How about meeting early morning, say 8ish? That way we could get there before the crowds. I could pick you up as I have a parking pass.

Let me know if you're free – hope you can make it.

All for now,
Sonia

Hi Sonia,

Lovely to hear from you – I've been meaning to get in touch for ages! Sorry for the delay in replying but life has been frantic recently! I've just started a new job – will tell you all about it when I see you. Thanks so much for the invitation – it would be great to meet up and the leisure centre sounds brilliant. Let's go for 16th, and thanks also for the offer of a lift – much appreciated.

All's well here, no major news apart from the new job. See you on 16th and look forward to catching up!

Liz

2 Find words and phrases in exercise 1 which mean ...

1 We haven't been in contact for a long time.
2 My life is still busy.
3 I'm writing to you ...
4 If that's not possible ...
5 Around eight o'clock.
6 I've been intending to write for a long time.
7 Sorry I didn't reply sooner.
8 I've been extremely busy.
9 Nothing special has happened recently.
10 Looking forward to exchanging news.

LANGUAGE FOCUS

Invitations & responses

1 Complete the expressions with the words from the box.

seeing	fancy	get	invitation	make	could
meet	shall	give	great	free	love

1 Sounds __________!
2 Do you __________ going out for a meal?
3 Let me know if you are __________.
4 We __________ meet outside Bailey's.
5 Would you like to __________ up for lunch?
6 Thanks very much for the __________.
7 Hope you can __________ it.
8 Look forward to __________ you then.
9 It would be great to __________ together.
10 I could __________ you a lift if you like.
11 I'd __________ to but I'm afraid I'm busy on Weds.
12 What time __________ I come round?

2 Decide who would have written the expressions in exercise 2, a, b or c.

a) The person making the invitation
b) The person responding to the invitation
c) Either

WRITING

1 Write an email to a friend, inviting them to take part in, or watch, a sporting event (125–175 words). Follow this format:

- Give details of the event.
- Suggest a time and place to meet.
- Give some personal news.

2 Write a response to the email (75–125 words). Follow this format:

- Thank the friend for the invitation.
- Confirm the arrangements.
- Give some personal news.
- Remember to start and end the emails in a suitable way.

4A | WRITING A narrative

LANGUAGE FOCUS

Using narrative tenses

1 Complete the text using an appropriate form of the verb in brackets (past simple, past continuous, past perfect simple or past perfect continuous).

It (1) _____________ (*pour*) with rain on a dark winter's night, and Robin (2) _____________ (*make*) his way home along the motorway. Earlier that day he (3) _____________ (*drive*) to London and (4) _____________ (*spend*) all day in a business meeting. Now he (5) _____________ (*drive*) for three hours and (6) _____________ (*feel*) tired, and ready for a good night's sleep. Arriving at a motorway service station, he (7) _____________ (*pull*) into the petrol station, (8) _____________ (*fill*) up his tank, and (9) _____________ (*go*) up to the till to pay. As he (10) _____________ (*stand*) in the queue, he (11) _____________ (*put*) his hand into his pocket and (12) _____________ (*realize*) to his horror that he (13) _____________ (*leave*) his credit card at the restaurant in London where he (14) _____________ (*have*) lunch. Wondering how he was going to get out of the situation, he suddenly (15) _____________ (*hear*) someone behind him say, 'Don't worry, Robin, this one is on me.' He (16) _____________ (*turn*) round and, to his great astonishment, (17) _____________ (*find*) himself face to face with his old friend Max, whom he (18) _____________ (*not/see*) since university days. The two men (19) _____________ (*burst*) out laughing and, when they (20) _____________ (*get*) over their surprise, (21) _____________ (*sit*) down to exchange news of their lives over cups of coffee.

Linking events

2 Complete the second sentence so that it means the same as the first.

1 He set off and immediately realized he had left his mobile phone behind.
He had just _______________________________.

2 Robin had driven 300km and was feeling tired.
Having _______________________________.

3 He put his hand in his pocket and discovered he had no money.
He put his hand in his pocket, only _______________.

4 He realized he had no money, and wondered what to do.
Realizing _______________________________.

5 He left London and immediately it started to rain.
No sooner _______________________________.

3 Complete the text with the words from the box.

as	when	on	who	just then

I'd been driving around for hours trying to find the hotel (1) ________ I found myself right in front of it. (2) ________ entering, I went over to the reception desk and spoke to the receptionist, (3) ________ informed me that there was no single room booked under my name. (4) ________ I was wondering what was going on, a man at the desk suddenly shrieked out loud and shouted, 'Jeffrey!' I hesitated for a few seconds and then realized that it was an old school friend who I hadn't seen for over 20 years. (5) ________ the receptionist announced that there was no single room booked under my name because the boss had in fact upgraded me to the luxury double room!

Describing emotion

4 Insert these expressions into the text in exercise 3.

to my astonishment	to my relief
to my delight	to my dismay

5 Match the sentence beginnings 1–5 in column A to the endings a–e in column B.

A

1 I realized to my utter dismay
2 Somewhat to my annoyance
3 To my great relief
4 I watched in complete bemusement
5 Imagine my fury

B

☐ a as the train passed by without stopping.
☐ b the river did not flood near my house.
☐ c that we would not catch our flight.
☐ d when I found that someone had stolen my laptop.
☐ e the man behind me jumped the queue.

6 Complete the sentences with your own ideas.

1 On opening my suitcase I discovered to my horror that
_______________________________.

2 Reading the letter, I learned to my delight that _______
_______________________________.

3 Imagine my disappointment when I arrived at the airport and found that _______________________.

4 I gazed in amusement as my neighbour's toddler _____
_______________________________.

4B | WRITING A description

READING

1 Read the description of a visit to Marrakech in Morocco. Was it mainly a positive or negative experience?

I have just spent two unforgettable days in Marrakech. To get there, I spent a few hours riding the Marrakech Express and watching the coastal plains rise in gentle undulations, scattered with patches of vibrantly coloured wild flowers, to become the snow-capped High Atlas Mountains that form the backdrop to the town.

Marrakech is an inland African town of pink mud buildings, fragrant and bustling markets and a square that attracts a dazzling array of human types. There were men of all ages wearing bright turquoise, ochre and shocking-pink hooded kaftans; local leather-jacketed youths; veiled women pulling at your sleeve and clamouring to henna your hands; toothless old men telling stories; stall-holders selling fresh orange juice or sizzling sheep's brains; groups of musicians from the mountains playing strange-looking instruments and dancing in circles; snake charmers and men with monkeys entertaining the crowds; Berbers in traditional red and yellow folk costumes touting themselves for photographs and couples strolling around looking unavoidably like tourists.

As the evening grew chilly, I retreated to my sprawling old budget hotel. I climbed to the roof terrace and watched the sun set over the pink town in a pink sky casting pink reflections on the mountains, and felt suddenly aware of the multiplicity of the ways of humankind on this planet, and yet its essential unity. I ate a meal of hearty Moroccan stew, and retreated to bed exhausted. The next day I arrived back home with my head spinning and my senses saturated.

2 Decide whether the statements are true (T) or false (F). Underline evidence from the description to support your answers.

1 Marrakech is overlooked by mountains. _____
2 Marrakech is on the coast. _____
3 The town square is a focus of human activity. _____
4 The writer was staying in a luxury hotel. _____
5 The writer had an intense experience on the roof terrace. _____
6 The writer returned home with vivid impressions of the visit. _____

LANGUAGE FOCUS

The five senses

1 Underline details in the text relating to the five senses.

1 Sound (eg *women clamouring*)
2 Smell (eg *fragrant markets*)
3 Touch (eg *women pulling at your sleeve*)
4 Taste (eg *fresh orange juice*)
5 Sight/colour (eg *vibrantly coloured flowers*)

Participle phrases

2 Rearrange the words to make phrases.

1 ages all of men kaftans wearing
2 your clamouring your hands women sleeve veiled at and to pulling henna
3 telling men toothless stories old
4 orange stall-holders or sizzling juice sheep's brains fresh selling
5 in musicians instruments playing dancing of strange-looking circles and groups
6 snake charmers crowds the entertaining
7 photographs for themselves touting Berbers
8 around looking like strolling unavoidably couples tourists

WRITING

1 Write a description of a visit to a crowded place (eg an airport, a park, a beach or a city square). Follow this format:

Paragraph 1: Locate the description. Where exactly is it? When and how did you go there?
Paragraph 2: Describe the people you saw. What did they look like? What were they doing? Use participle phrases, and phrases relating to the five senses. Begin 'There were …'
Paragraph 3: What happened at the end? How did you feel, and what impressions were you left with?

5A | WRITING A letter of complaint

LANGUAGE FOCUS

Explaining the results of problems

1 Complete the sentences with the phrases from the box (sometimes more than one alternative is possible).

so that	which constitutes	as a result
which means	which makes	which is

1 The bathroom radiator is not working __________ the temperature is freezing.
2 The walls are paper thin, __________ that you can hear every noise the neighbours make.
3 The walls are damp, __________ a health hazard.
4 The doorbell isn't working, and __________ visitors have to bang on the door.
5 The lift is out of order, __________ extremely annoying, as I have to walk up three flights of stairs.
6 The taps keep dripping, __________ it difficult to get to sleep at night.

2 Look at the picture and write sentences to describe the problems in the flat.

1 ______________________________.
2 ______________________________.
3 ______________________________.
4 ______________________________.
5 ______________________________.
6 ______________________________.

3 Write sentences to explain the results of the problems in exercise 2. Use words and phrases from the box and from exercise 1.

a health hazard	do the washing up
go to the launderette	a safety hazard
extremely uncomfortable	draughty

1 ______________________________.
2 ______________________________.
3 ______________________________.
4 ______________________________.
5 ______________________________.
6 ______________________________.

Articles

4 Add *a*/*an* or *the* to the letter where necessary.

Hi Jan
Thanks very much for postcard you sent from Spain. Glad to hear you enjoyed holiday. You deserved it.
Just thought I'd write to let you know that we've moved into new flat on second floor in modern apartment block quite close to city centre. Block is in quiet residential area near to park, and we are very happy here. But there are some problems with flat. Kitchen is very small and cooker is a bit erratic, which means that we can't always eat at home. Also, carpet in hall is stained and filthy and we've asked landlord to have it cleaned. When we first moved in, toilet didn't flush. Luckily, landlord sent plumber round to fix it straight away.
Anyway, on the whole things are working out OK. You must come round to visit sometime!
That's all for now
Kate

5 Match each use of *the* in exercise 4 to the explanations 1–6.

1 ordinal nouns
2 something that has been mentioned before
3 an attribute of something mentioned before
4 normally only one in a place
5 specified or defined
6 known to the reader

5B | WRITING A letter of thanks

READING

1 Read the letter. What is the writer's purpose?

Dear Mr and Mrs Burd,

I am writing on behalf of the Race For Schools team to thank you for your very generous sponsorship of our runners in last Sunday's race in aid of schools in Africa. The event was a great success and we managed to raise a magnificent total of €87,215 which will go towards buying books for underprivileged children in developing countries. Thankfully the rain held off during the afternoon, and the runners and spectators were all in good spirits for the event.

The turnout this year was excellent and the participants managed to complete the 5km in record times. We have been overwhelmed by the donations we have received this year in response to our sponsorship appeal. But for the generosity of supporters like you we would not be able to go on funding our educational projects in Africa. With your help we are able to really make a difference to many many children's lives.

With thanks once again,

Yours sincerely,

Tess Nowell

2 Choose the correct alternative to complete the sentences.

1 Tess Nowell *organized* / *sponsored* the race.
2 The proceeds of the race will go to *local schools* / *an educational charity*.
3 The weather was *rainy* / *dry* during the race.
4 *Many runners* / *Record numbers of runners* took part in the race.
5 The amount raised this year was *more* / *less* than expected.
6 Race for Schools *can* / *cannot* continue funding educational projects.
7 Race for Schools *can* / *cannot* manage without charitable contributions.

LANGUAGE FOCUS

Expressions of thanks

1 Match the letter extracts 1–6 in column A to the topics a–f in column B.

A

1 Just a brief note to say thank you for putting me up while I was in Dublin last week.

2 I am writing to say how much Bob and I appreciate the hard work you put into helping make Jeremy's 21st such a success last Saturday.

3 I am writing to extend our sincere thanks for the generous cheque you sent in response to our appeal for guide dogs for the blind.

4 Thank you so much for the beautiful set of mugs you gave to Tony and me.

5 This is just to say a big thank you for your kind words when I was feeling so down last night.

6 I am writing to express my gratitude for the scholarship you have awarded me.

B

☐ a A wedding present
☐ b Emotional support
☐ c Hospitality
☐ d Help with a party
☐ e Educational funding
☐ f A charitable donation

Explaining why you are grateful

2 Complete the sentences with the words from the box.

Thanks	But	With	If	Without

1 __________ for your guidance and advice I would not have known what to do.
2 __________ extra tuition I was able to pass the exam.
3 __________ it hadn't been for your financial backing we would not have been able to stage the play.
4 __________ to your hard work we managed to get the house ready on time.
5 __________ your support I don't know how I would have managed.

WRITING

1 Write a letter of thanks to someone for offering hospitality or tuition to a group of visiting students. Use expressions from Language focus exercises 1 and 2.

Follow this format:
Paragraph 1: State the purpose of the letter.
Paragraph 2: Give details of what happened.
Paragraph 3: Say why you are grateful.

6A | WRITING An essay (1)

LANGUAGE FOCUS

Expressing a viewpoint

1 Rearrange the words to make sentences.

1 case play simply instrument the a that not can it learn is to anyone musical

____.

2 should that the personally arts the believe government I subsidize

____.

3 is true it audience probably to that minority ballet a attracts say

____.

4 that the is sake their for generally arts are important it agreed own

____.

5 great lives dispute that would enriches fact people's the no one art

____.

6 for has innate whether everyone would personally talent I an art question

____.

2 Say whether the statements 1–6 represent ...

a) a strong claim or commonly held view.
b) a personal opinion.

1 It is widely believed that watching too much television can have a harmful effect on children.
2 All the evidence suggests that many people would like to go out more to arts events.
3 I would argue that the arts should be publicly funded.
4 It is often claimed that modern art has no aesthetic value.
5 There can be no doubt that Shakespeare is Britain's greatest playwright.
6 It is my view that some form of censorship is necessary.

Arguing against a viewpoint

3 Complete the sentences expressing a viewpoint by adding one word.

1 There are who argue that television is dumbing down our culture.
2 Of, schools can sometimes stifle creativity.
3 Opponents censorship argue that it should not interfere with freedom of expression in the arts.
4 Is true that much modern art is not easy to understand.
5 Of public funding of the arts claim that museums and art galleries should not charge an entrance fee.

4 Match the viewpoints 1–5 in exercise 3 to the opposite view a–e.

☐ a However, it is becoming increasingly difficult to maintain the current level of services without an additional source of income.
☐ b But surely that does not mean it does not deserve to be called art?
☐ c However, it could also be argued that the capacity for self-expression is not the main aim of education.
☐ d But others believe that entertainment is an important function of public broadcasting.
☐ e But surely there is also a need to protect children from explicit violent or sexual content?

5 Write two sentences on each of the following topics, a) expressing a viewpoint and b) arguing against it.

1 Buying an original painting

a) ____.

b) ____.

2 Hollywood films

a) ____.

b) ____.

6B | WRITING An essay (2)

READING

1 Read the essay on GM foods. Is the writer mainly for or against their use?

(1) ___________ there have been enormous scientific advances in the production of genetically modified (GM) foods. However, (2) ___________ GM foods are beneficial to humanity is a highly controversial one. In many European countries vigorous campaigns by anti-GM protesters have led to an unofficial moratorium on the growth and import of GM crops.

(3) ___________ they offer a number of benefits. First, crops can be engineered so as to be resistant to pests, thus reducing the need for pesticides. Second, they can be grown in poor conditions and thus contribute to combating world hunger. (4) ___________, GM technology can bring about improvements in the flavour and shelf life of the food we eat.

However, (5) ___________ they may be detrimental to our health in ways of which we are not yet aware. (6) ___________ they can be accidentally spread by winds, thus infecting neighbouring crops. (7) ___________, anti-GM campaigners point out that large businesses may develop monopolies on the production of GM crops, driving smaller producers out of business.

My own view is that, (8) ___________ GM foods offer an important solution to the problem of hunger in developing countries. (9) ___________ more research needs to be done into possible risks to health before they are developed on a large scale.

2 Choose the correct alternative to describe GM foods.

1 They may be *more* / *less* affected by pests.
2 They may *increase* / *reduce* world hunger.
3 They may be on sale for a *shorter* / *longer* time in shops.
4 They may be *beneficial* / *harmful* to our health.
5 They may *affect* / *be affected by* nearby crops.
6 They may *increase* / *reduce* financial competition.

3 Complete the essay with words and phrases from the box.

on balance   critics fear that   finally   however   lastly
the question of whether   a further problem is that
supporters of GM foods contend that   in recent decades

LANGUAGE FOCUS

Result clauses

1 Complete the sentences with result clauses from the essay.

1 Crops can be engineered so as to be resistant to pests, ___________________________________.

2 They can be grown in poor conditions, ___________________________________.

3 They can be accidentally spread by winds, ___________________________________.

4 Large businesses may develop monopolies on the production of GM crops, ___________________________________.

2 Complete the sentence beginnings 1–4 in column A with the endings a–d in column B.

A

1 The shelf life of GM foods can be extended,
2 The use of pesticides can be reduced,
3 Anti-GM protesters have campaigned vigorously,
4 GM foods may pose health risks,

B

☐ a thus reducing the risk to the environment.
☐ b raising the public's awareness of the issue.
☐ c and thus bring about harmful side effects of which we are as yet unaware.
☐ d thus offering financial benefits to retailers.

WRITING

1 Write an essay on a) computerization, b) space travel or c) the teaching of science in schools. Follow this format:

Paragraph 1: Introduce the topic. Say why it is controversial.
Paragraph 2: Introduce arguments in favour. Use result clauses.
Paragraph 3: Introduce arguments against. Use result clauses.
Paragraph 4: Give your own opinion, with reasons.

The Rough Crossing

by F Scott Fitzgerald

I

Once on the long, covered piers, you have come into a ghostly country that is no longer Here and not yet There. Especially at night. There is a hazy yellow vault full of shouting, echoing voices. There is the rumble of trucks and the clump of trunks, the strident chatter of a crane and the first salt smell of the sea. You hurry through, even though there's time. The past, the continent, is behind you; the future is that glowing mouth in the side of the ship; this dim turbulent alley is too confusedly the present.

Up the gangplank, and the vision of the world adjusts itself, narrows. One is a citizen of a commonwealth smaller than Andorra[1]. One is no longer so sure of anything. Curiously unmoved the men at the purser's desk, cell-like the cabin, disdainful the eyes of voyagers and their friends, solemn the officer who stands on the deserted promenade deck thinking something of his own as he stares at the crowd below. A last odd idea that one didn't really have to come, then the loud, mournful whistles, and the thing – certainly not the boat, but rather a human idea, a frame of mind – pushes forth into the big dark night.

Adrian Smith, one of the celebrities on board – not a very great celebrity, but important enough to be bathed in flashlight by a photographer who had been given his name, but wasn't sure what his subject 'did' – Adrian Smith and his blonde wife, Eva, went up to the promenade deck, passed the melancholy ship's officer, and, finding a quiet aerie[2], put their elbows on the rail.

'We're going!' he cried presently, and they both laughed in ecstasy. 'We've escaped. They can't get us now.'

'Who?'

He waved his hand vaguely at the civic tiara[3].

'All those people out there. They'll come with their posses[4] and their warrants and list of crimes we've committed, and ring the bell at our door on Park Avenue[5] and ask for the Adrian Smiths, but what ho! the Adrian Smiths and their children and nurse are off for France.'

'You make me think we really have committed crimes.'

'They can't have you,' he said frowning. 'That's one thing they're after me about – they know I haven't got any right to a person like you, and they're furious. That's one reason I'm glad to get away.'

'Darling,' said Eva.

She was twenty-six – five years younger than he. She was something precious to everyone who knew her.

'I like this boat better than the *Majestic* or the *Aquitania*,' she remarked, unfaithful to the ships that had served their honeymoon.

'It's much smaller.'

'But it's very slick and it has all those little shops along the corridors. And I think the staterooms are bigger.'

'The people are very formal – did you notice? – as if they thought everyone else was a card sharp[6]. And in about four days half of them will be calling the other half by their first names.'

Four of the people came by now – a quartet of young girls abreast, making a circuit of the deck. Their eight eyes swept momentarily towards Adrian and Eva, and then swept automatically back, save for one pair which lingered for an instant with a little start. They belonged to one of the girls in the middle, who was, indeed, the only passenger of the four. She was not more than eighteen – a dark little beauty with the fine crystal gloss over her that, in brunettes, takes the place of a blonde's bright glow.

'Now, who's that?' wondered Adrian. 'I've seen her before.'

'She's pretty,' said Eva.

'Yes.' He kept wondering, and Eva deferred momentarily to his distraction; then, smiling up at him, she drew him back into their privacy.

'Tell me more,' she said.

'About what?'

'About us – what a good time we'll have, and how we'll be much better and happier, and very close always.'

'How could we be any closer?' His arm pulled her to him.

'But I mean never even quarrel any more about silly things. You know, I made up my mind when you gave me my birthday present last week' – her fingers caressed the fine seed pearls at her throat – 'that I'd try never to say a mean thing to you again.'

'You never have, my precious.'

Yet even as he strained her against his side she knew that the moment of utter isolation had passed almost before it had begun. His antennae were already out, feeling over this new world.

'Most of the people look rather awful,' he said – 'little and swarthy and ugly. Americans didn't use to look like that.'

'They look dreary,' she agreed. 'Let's not get to know anybody, but just stay together.'

A gong was beating now, and stewards were shouting down the decks, 'Visitors ashore, please!' and voices rose to a strident chorus. For a while the gangplanks were thronged; then they were empty, and the jostling crowd behind the barrier waved and called unintelligible things, and kept up a grin of good will. As the stevedores began to work at the ropes a flat-faced, somewhat befuddled young man arrived in a great hurry and was assisted up the gangplank by a porter and a taxi driver. The ship having swallowed him as impassively as though he were a missionary for Beirut[7], a low, portentous vibration began. The pier with its faces commenced to slide by, and for a moment the boat was just a piece accidentally split off from it; then the faces became remote, voiceless, and the pier was one among many yellow blurs along the water front. Now the harbour flowed swiftly toward the sea.

On a northern parallel of latitude a hurricane was forming and moving south by southeast preceded by a strong west wind. On its course it was destined to swamp the *Peter I. Eudin* of Amsterdam, with a crew of sixty-six, to break a boom on the largest boat in the world, and to bring grief and want to the wives of several hundred seamen. This liner, leaving New York Sunday evening, would enter the zone of the storm Tuesday, and of the hurricane late Wednesday night.

II

Tuesday afternoon Adrian and Eva paid their first visit to the smoking-room. This was not in accord with their intentions – they had 'never wanted to see a cocktail again' after leaving America – but they had forgotten the staccato loneliness of ships, and all activity centred about the bar. So they went in for just a minute.

1 a small country bordered by Spain and France in the Pyrenees (the mountain chain on the Spanish-French border)

2 *US*: in British English, *eyrie* – a place that is very high and difficult to reach; the nest built by an eagle

3 a piece of jewellery a woman wears on top of her head on a formal occasion, it is semicircular and looks like a crown. Used here to describe the crowd, which was probably standing in a semicircle

4 *US, informal:* in the past, a group of ordinary men gathered together by a law officer to search for a criminal

5 a wide street in Manhattan, New York City. It is one of the most expensive and prestigious addresses in New York

6 a professional card player who cheats to win money

7 the capital city of Lebanon. At the turn of the 20th century Beirut was a centre of missionary activity

It was full. There were those who had been there since luncheon[8], and those who would be there until dinner, not to mention a faithful few who had been there since nine this morning. It was a prosperous assembly, taking its recreation at bridge[9], solitaire[10], detective stories, alcohol, argument and love. Up to this point you could have matched it in the club or casino life of any country, but over it all played a repressed nervous energy, a barely disguised impatience that extended to old and young alike. The cruise had begun, and they had enjoyed the beginning, but the show was not varied enough to last six days, and already they wanted it to be over.

At a table near them Adrian saw the pretty girl who had stared at him on the deck the first night. Again he was fascinated by her loveliness; there was no mist upon the brilliant gloss that gleamed through the smoky confusion of the room. He and Eva had decided from the passenger list that she was probably 'Miss Elizabeth D'Amido and maid', and he had heard her called Betsy as he walked past a deck-tennis game. Among the young people with her was the flat-nosed youth who had been 'poured on board', the night of their departure; yesterday he had walked the deck morosely, but he was apparently reviving. Miss D'Amido whispered something to him, and he looked over at the Smiths with curious eyes. Adrian was new enough at being a celebrity to turn self-consciously away.

'There's a little roll. Do you feel it?' Eva demanded.

'Perhaps we'd better split a pint of champagne.'

While he gave the order a short colloquy[11] was taking place at the other table; presently a young man rose and came over to them.

'Isn't this Mr Adrian Smith?'

'Yes.'

'We wondered if we couldn't put you down for the deck-tennis tournament. We're going to have a deck-tennis tournament.'

'Why –' Adrian hesitated.

'My name's Stacomb,' burst out the young man. 'We all know your – your plays or whatever it is, and all that – and we wondered if you wouldn't like to come over to our table.'

Somewhat overwhelmed, Adrian laughed: Mr Stacomb, glib, soft, slouching, waited; evidently under the impression that he had delivered himself of a graceful compliment.

Adrian, understanding that, too, replied: 'Thanks, but perhaps you'd better come over here.'

'We've got a bigger table.'

'But we're older and more – more settled.'

The young man laughed kindly, as if to say, 'That's all right.'

'Put me down,' said Adrian. 'How much do I owe you?'

'One buck[12]. Call me Stac.'

'Why?' asked Adrian, startled.

'It's shorter.'

When he had gone they smiled broadly.

'Heavens,' Eva gasped, 'I believe they are coming over.'

They were. With a great draining of glasses, calling of waiters, shuffling of chairs, three boys and two girls moved to the Smiths' table. If there was any diffidence, it was confined to the hosts; for the new additions gathered around them eagerly, eyeing Adrian with respect – too much respect – as if to say: 'This was probably a mistake and won't be amusing, but maybe we'll get something out of it to help us in our after life, like at school[13].'

In a moment Miss D'Amido changed seats with one of the men and placed her radiant self at Adrian's side, looking at him with manifest admiration.

'I fell in love with you the minute I saw you,' she said audibly and without self-consciousness; 'so I'll take all the blame for butting in. I've seen your play four times.'

Adrian called a waiter to take their orders.

'You see,' continued Miss D'Amido, 'we're going into a storm, and you might be prostrated[14] the rest of the trip, so I couldn't take any chances.'

He saw that there was no undertone or innuendo in what she said, nor the need of any. The words themselves were enough, and the deference with which she neglected the young men and bent her politeness on him was somehow very touching. A little glow went over him; he was having rather more than a pleasant time.

Eva was less entertained; but the flat-nosed young man, whose name was Butterworth, knew people that she did, and that seemed to make the affair less careless and casual. She did not like meeting new people unless they had 'something to contribute', and she was often bored by the great streams of them, of all types and conditions and classes, that passed through Adrian's life. She herself 'had everything' – which is to say that she was well endowed with talents and with charm – and the mere novelty of people did not seem a sufficient reason for eternally offering everything up to them.

Half an hour later when she rose to go and see the children, she was content that the episode was over. It was colder on deck, with a damp that was almost rain, and there was a perceptible motion. Opening the door of her stateroom she was surprised to find the cabin steward sitting languidly on her bed, his head slumped upon the upright pillow. He looked at her listlessly as she came in, but made no move to get up.

'When you've finished your nap you can fetch me a new pillow-case,' she said briskly.

Still the man didn't move. She perceived then that his face was green.

'You can't be seasick in here,' she announced firmly. 'You go and lie down in your own quarters.'

'It's me[15] side,' he said faintly. He tried to rise, gave out a little rasping sound of pain and sank back again. Eva rang for the stewardess.

A steady pitch, toss, roll had begun in earnest and she felt no sympathy for the steward, but only wanted to get him out as quick as possible. It was outrageous for a member of the crew to be seasick. When the stewardess came in Eva tried to explain this, but now her own head was whirring, and throwing herself on the bed, she covered her eyes.

'It's his fault,' she groaned when the man was assisted from the room. 'I was all right and it made me sick to look at him. I wish he'd die.'

In a few minutes Adrian came in.

'Oh, but I'm sick!' she cried.

'Why, you poor baby.' He leaned over and took her in his arms. 'Why didn't you tell me?'

'I was all right upstairs, but there was a steward – Oh, I'm too sick to talk.'

'You'd better have dinner in bed.'

8 *formal:* lunch, especially a formal lunch for a lot of people
9 a card game for four players who play in two teams. It was very popular at the beginning of the 20th century and often associated with the upper classes
10 *mainly US:* a card game played by one person, called *patience* in British English
11 *formal, rare:* a dialogue or conference
12 *US, informal:* a dollar
13 *US, informal:* a college or university
14 *formal:* extremely upset or ill
15 *non-standard spoken English:* my

'Dinner! Oh, my heavens!'

He waited solicitously, but she wanted to hear his voice, to have it drown out the complaining sound of the beams.

'Where've you been?'

'Helping to sign up people for the tournament.'

'Will they have it if it's like this? Because if they do I'll just lose for you.'

He didn't answer; opening her eyes, she saw that he was frowning.

'I didn't know you were going in the doubles,' he said.

'Why, that's the only fun.'

'I told the D'Amido girl I'd play with her.'

'Oh.'

'I didn't think. You know I'd much rather play with you.'

'Why didn't you, then?' she asked coolly.

'It never occurred to me.'

She remembered that on their honeymoon they had been in the finals and won a prize. Years passed. But Adrian never frowned in this regretful way unless he felt a little guilty. He stumbled about, getting his dinner clothes out of the trunk, and she shut her eyes.

When a particular violent lurch startled her awake again he was dressed and tying his tie. He looked healthy and fresh, and his eyes were bright.

'Well, how about it?' he inquired. 'Can you make it, or no?'

'No.'

'Can I do anything for you before I go?'

'Where are you going?'

'Meeting those kids in the bar. Can I do anything for you?'

'No.'

'Darling, I hate to leave you like this.'

'Don't be silly. I just want to sleep.'

That solicitous frown – when she knew he was crazy to be out and away from the close cabin. She was glad when the door closed. The thing to do was to sleep, sleep.

Up – down – sideways. Hey there, not so far! Pull her round the corner there! Now roll her, right – left – Crea-eak![16] Wrench! Swoop!

Some hours later Eva was dimly conscious of Adrian bending over her. She wanted him to put his arms around her and draw her up out of this dizzy lethargy, but by the time she was fully awake the cabin was empty. He had looked in and gone. When she awoke next the cabin was dark and he was in bed.

The morning was fresh and cool, and the sea was just enough calmer to make Eva think she could get up. They breakfasted in the cabin and with Adrian's help she accomplished an unsatisfactory makeshift toilet[17] and they went up on the boat deck. The tennis tournament had already begun and was furnishing action for a dozen amateur movie cameras, but the majority of passengers were represented by lifeless bundles in deck chairs beside untasted trays.

Adrian and Miss D'Amido played their first match. She was deft and graceful; blatantly well. There was even more warmth behind her ivory skin than there had been the day before. The strolling first officer stopped and talked to her; half a dozen men whom she couldn't have known three days ago called her Betsy. She was already the pretty girl of the voyage, the cynosure[18] of starved ship's eyes.

But after a while Eva preferred to watch the gulls in the wireless masts and the slow slide of the roll-top sky. Most of the passengers looked silly with their movie cameras that they had all rushed to get and now didn't know what to use for, but the sailors painting the lifeboat stanchions were quiet and beaten and sympathetic, and probably wished, as she did, that the voyage was over.

Butterworth sat down on the deck beside her chair.

'They're operating on one of the stewards this morning. Must be terrible in this sea.'

'Operating? What for?' she asked listlessly.

'Appendicitis[19]. They have to operate now because we're going into worse weather. That's why they're having the ship's party tonight.'

'Oh, the poor man!' she cried, realizing it must be her steward.

Adrian was showing off now by being very courteous and thoughtful in the game.

'Sorry. Did you hurt yourself? ... No, it was my fault ... You better put on your coat right away, partner, or you'll catch cold.'

The match was over and they had won. Flushed and hearty, he came up to Eva's chair.

'How do you feel?'

'Terrible.'

'Winners are buying a drink in the bar,' he said apologetically.

'I'm coming, too,' Eva said, but an immediate dizziness made her sink back in her chair.

'You'd better stay here. I'll send you up something.'

She felt that his public manner had hardened towards her slightly.

'You'll come back?'

'Oh, right away.'

She was alone on the boat deck, save for a solitary ship's officer who slanted obliquely as he paced the bridge. When the cocktail arrived she forced herself to drink it, and felt better. Trying to distract her mind with pleasant things, she reached back to the sanguine talks that she and Adrian had had before sailing: There was the little villa in Brittany[20], the children learning French – that was all she could think of now – the little villa in Brittany, the children learning French – so she repeated the words over and over to herself until they became as meaningless as the wide white sky. The why of their being here had suddenly eluded her; she felt unmotivated, accidental, and she wanted Adrian to come back quick, all responsive and tender, to reassure her. It was in the hope that there was some secret of graceful living, some real compensation for the lost, careless confidence of twenty-one, that they were going to spend a year in France.

The day passed darkly, with fewer people around and a wet sky falling. Suddenly it was five o'clock, and they were all in the bar again, and Mr Butterworth was telling her about his past. She took a good deal of champagne, but she was seasick dimly through it, as if the illness was her soul trying to struggle up through some thickening incrustation of abnormal life.

'You're my idea of a Greek goddess, physically,' Butterworth was saying.

It was pleasant to be Mr Butterworth's idea of a Greek goddess physically, but where was Adrian? He and Miss D'Amido had gone out on a forward deck to feel the spray. Eva heard herself promising to get out her colours and paint the Eiffel Tower[21] on Butterworth's shirt front for the party tonight.

When Adrian and Betsy D'Amido, soaked with spray, opened the door with difficulty against the driving wind and came into the now-covered security of the promenade deck, they stopped and turned toward each other.

---

16 non-standard spelling used to illustrate the sound

17 *formal*: the process of washing and getting dressed

18 *formal*: someone or something that is a centre of attention and admiration, often because they are beautiful or brilliant

19 *medical*: an illness in which your appendix becomes infected and has to be removed in a medical operation

20 a region in the north-west of France

21 a famous landmark in Paris

'Well?' she said. But he only stood with his back to the rail, looking at her, afraid to speak. She was silent, too, because she wanted him to be first; so for a moment nothing happened. Then she made a step towards him, and he took her in his arms and kissed her forehead.

'You're just sorry for me, that's all.' She began to cry a little. 'You're just being kind.'

'I feel terribly about it.' His voice was taut and trembling.

'Then kiss me.'

The deck was empty. He bent over her swiftly.

'No, really kiss me.'

He could not remember when anything had felt so young and fresh as her lips. The rain lay, like tears shed for him, upon the softly shining porcelain cheeks. She was all new and immaculate, and her eyes were wild.

'I love you,' she whispered. 'I can't help loving you, can I? When I first saw you – oh, not on the boat, but over a year ago – Grace Heally took me to a rehearsal and suddenly you jumped up in the second row and began telling them what to do. I wrote you a letter and tore it up.'

'We've got to go.'

She was weeping as they walked along the deck. Once more, imprudently, she held up her face to him at the door of her cabin. His blood was beating through him in wild tumult as he walked on to the bar.

He was thankful that Eva scarcely seemed to notice him or to know that he had been gone. After a moment he pretended an interest in what she was doing.

'What's that?'

'She's painting the Eiffel Tower on my shirt front for tonight,' explained Butterworth.

'There,' Eva laid away her brush and wiped her hands.

'How's that?'

'A *chef-d'oeuvre*[22].'

Her eyes swept around the watching group, lingered casually upon Adrian.

'You're wet. Go and change.'

'You come too.'

'I want another champagne cocktail.'

'You've had enough. It's time to dress for the party.'

Unwilling she closed her paints and preceded him.

'Stacomb's got a table for nine,' he remarked as they walked along the corridor.

'The younger set,' she said with unnecessary bitterness. 'Oh, the younger set. And you just having the time of your life – with a child.'

They had a long discussion in the cabin, unpleasant on her part and evasive on his, which ended when the ship gave a sudden gigantic heave, and Eva, the edge worn off her champagne, felt ill again. There was nothing to do but to have a cocktail in the cabin, and after that they decided to go to the party – she believed him now, or she didn't care.

Adrian was ready first – he never wore fancy dress.

'I'll go on up. Don't be long.'

'Wait for me, please; it's rocking so.'

He sat down on a bed, concealing his impatience.

'You don't mind waiting, do you? I don't want to parade up there all alone.'

She was taking a tuck in an oriental costume rented from the barber.

'Ships make people feel crazy,' she said. 'I think they're awful.'

'Yes,' he muttered absently.

'When it gets very bad I pretend I'm in the top of a tree, rocking to and fro. But finally I get pretending everything, and finally I have to pretend I'm sane when I know I'm not.'

'If you get thinking that way you will go crazy.'

'Look, Adrian.' She held up the string of pearls before clasping them on. 'Aren't they lovely?'

In Adrian's impatience she seemed to move around the cabin like a figure in a slow-motion picture[23]. After a moment he demanded:

'Are you going to be long? It's stifling in here.'

'You go on!' she fired up.

'I don't want –'

'Go on, please! You just make me nervous trying to hurry me.'

With a show of reluctance he left her. After a moment's hesitation he went down a flight to a deck below and knocked at a door.

'Betsy.'

'Just a minute.'

She came out in the corridor attired in a red pea-jacket[24] and trousers borrowed from the elevator boy.

'Do elevator boys have fleas?' she demanded. 'I've got everything in the world on under this as a precaution.'

'I had to see you,' he said quickly.

'Careful,' she whispered. 'Mrs Worden, who's supposed to be chaperoning me, is across the way. She's sick.'

'I'm sick for you.'

They kissed suddenly, clung close together in the narrow corridor, swaying to and fro with the motion of the ship.

'Don't go away,' she murmured.

'I've got to. I've –'

Her youth seemed to flow into him, bearing him up into a delicate romantic ecstasy that transcended passion. He couldn't relinquish it; he had discovered something that he had thought was lost with his own youth forever. As he walked along the passage he knew that he had stopped thinking, no longer dared to think.

He met Eva going into the bar.

'Where've you been?' she asked with a strained smile.

'To see about the table.'

She was lovely; her cool distinction conquered the trite costume and filled him with a resurgence of approval and pride. They sat down at a table.

The gale was rising hour by hour and the mere traversing of a passage had become a rough matter. In every stateroom trunks were lashed to the washstands, and the *Vestris* disaster[25] was being reviewed in detail by nervous ladies, tossing, ill and wretched, upon their beds. In the smoking-room a stout gentleman had been hurled backward and suffered a badly cut head; and now the lighter chairs and tables were stacked and roped against the wall.

The crowd who had donned[26] fancy dress and were dining together had swollen to about sixteen. The only remaining qualification for membership was the ability to reach the smoking-room. They ranged from a Groton-Harvard[27] lawyer to an ungrammatical broker they had nicknamed Gyp the Blood[28], but distinctions had disappeared; for the moment they were samurai, chosen from several hundred for their triumphant resistance to the storm.

The gala dinner, overhung sardonically with lanterns and streamers, was interrupted by great communal slides across the

22 *French*: masterpiece
23 *mainly US*: film
24 a heavy jacket, made of wool, that was originally worn by sailors in Europe
25 in 1928 the ocean liner *SS Vestris* ran into a severe storm while on a voyage from New Jersey to Barbados. 65 passengers and 45 members of the crew died
26 *mainly literary*: put on clothes
27 who had been to Groton, an elite private school, and Harvard University
28 Harry Horowitz (1889–1914), better known as *Gyp the Blood*, was the leader of a notorious New York City gang in the early 20th century

room, precipitate retirements and spilled wine, while the ship roared and complained that under the panoply[29] of a palace it was a ship after all. Upstairs afterward a dozen couples tried to dance, shuffling and galloping here and there in a crazy fandango[30], thrust around fantastically by a will alien to their own. In view of the condition of tortured hundreds below, there grew to be something indecent about it like a revel[31] in a house of mourning, and presently there was an egress[32] of the ever-dwindling survivors towards the bar.

As the evening passed, Eva's feeling of unreality increased. Adrian had disappeared – presumably with Miss D'Amido – and her mind, distorted by illness and champagne, began to enlarge upon the fact; annoyance changed slowly to dark and brooding anger, grief to desperation. She had never tried to bind Adrian, never needed to – for they were serious people, with all sorts of mutual interests, and satisfied with each other – but this was a breach of the contract, this was cruel. How could he think that she didn't know?

It seemed several hours later that he leaned over her chair in the bar where she was giving some woman an impassioned lecture upon babies, and said:

'Eva, we'd better turn in[33].'

Her lip curled. 'So that you can leave me there and then come back to your eighteen-year –'

'Be quiet.'

'I won't come to bed.'

'Very well. Good night.'

More time passed and the people at the table changed. The stewards wanted to close up the room, and thinking of Adrian – her Adrian – off somewhere saying tender things to someone fresh and lovely, Eva began to cry.

'But he's gone to bed,' her last attendants assured her. 'We saw him go.'

She shook her head. She knew better. Adrian was lost. The long seven-year dream was broken. Probably she was punished for something she had done; as this thought occurred to her the shrieking timbers overhead began to mutter that she had guessed at last. This was for the selfishness to her mother, who hadn't wanted her to marry Adrian; for all the sins and omissions of her life. She stood up, saying she must go out and get some air.

The deck was dark and drenched with wind and rain. The ship pounded through valleys, fleeing from black mountains of water that roared towards it. Looking out at the night, Eva saw that there was no chance for them unless she could make atonement, propitiate[34] the storm. It was Adrian's love that was demanded of her. Deliberately she unclasped her pearl necklace, lifted it to her lips – for she knew that with it went the freshest, fairest part of her life – and flung it out into the gale.

III

When Adrian awoke it was lunchtime, but he knew that some heavier sound than the bugle[35] had called him up from his deep sleep. Then he realized that the trunk had broken loose from its lashings and was being thrown back and forth between a wardrobe and Eva's bed. With an exclamation he jumped up, but she was unharmed – still in costume and stretched out in deep sleep. When the steward had helped him secure the trunk, Eva opened a single eye.

'How are you?' he demanded, sitting on the side of her bed.

She closed the eye, opened it again.

'We're in a hurricane now,' he told her. 'The steward says it's the worst he's seen in twenty years.'

'My head,' she muttered. 'Hold my head.'

'How?'

'In front. My eyes are going out. I think I'm dying.'

'Nonsense. Do you want the doctor?'

She gave a funny little gasp that frightened him; he rang and sent the steward for the doctor.

The young doctor was pale and tired. There was a stubble of beard upon his face. He bowed curtly as he came in and, turning to Adrian, said with scant ceremony:

'What's the matter?'

'My wife doesn't feel well.'

'Well, what is it you want – a bromide[36]?'

A little annoyed by his shortness, Adrian said: 'You'd better examine her and see what she needs.'

'She needs a bromide,' said the doctor. 'I've given orders that she is not to have any more to drink on this ship.'

'Why not?' demanded Adrian in astonishment.

'Don't you know what happened last night?'

'Why, no, I was asleep.'

'Mrs Smith wandered around the boat for an hour, not knowing what she was doing. A sailor was sent to follow her, and then the medical stewardess tried to get her to bed, and your wife insulted her.'

'Oh, my heavens!' cried Eva faintly.

'The nurse and I had both been up all night with Steward Carton, who died this morning.' He picked up his case. 'I'll send down a bromide for Mrs Smith. Good-bye.'

For a few minutes there was silence in the cabin. Then Adrian put his arm around her quickly.

'Never mind,' he said. 'We'll straighten it out.'

'I remember now.' Her voice was an awed whisper. 'My pearls. I threw them overboard.'

'Threw them overboard!'

'Then I began looking for you.'

'But I was here in bed.'

'I didn't believe it; I thought you were with that girl.'

'She collapsed during dinner. I was taking a nap down here.'

Frowning, he rang the bell and asked the steward for luncheon and a bottle of beer.

'Sorry, but we can't serve any beer to your cabin, sir.'

When he went out Adrian exploded: 'This is an outrage. You were simply crazy from that storm and they can't be so high-handed. I'll see the captain.'

'Isn't that awful?' Eva murmured. 'The poor man died.'

She turned over and began to sob into her pillow. There was a knock at the door.

'Can I come in?'

The assiduous[37] Mr Butterworth, surprisingly healthy and immaculate, came into the crazily tipping cabin.

'Well, how's the mystic?' he demanded of Eva. 'Do you remember praying to the elements in the bar last night?'

'I don't want to remember anything about last night.'

---

29 *formal:* a large and impressive display
30 a fast dance from Spain
31 *mainly literary:* a lively and noisy party or celebration, especially where people sing, dance and drink alcohol
32 *very formal:* the action of leaving a place
33 *informal, old-fashioned:* to go to bed at night
34 *formal:* to try to stop someone from being angry with you by doing something to please them
35 a musical instrument sometimes used to show that an activity is about to begin or end
36 a drug to make people calm or help them to sleep
37 *formal:* hard-working and thorough

They told him about the stewardess, and with the telling the situation lightened; they all laughed together.

'I'm going to get you some beer to have with your luncheon,' Butterworth said. 'You ought to get up on deck.'

'Don't go,' Eva said. 'You look so cheerful and nice.'

'Just for ten minutes.'

When he had gone, Adrian rang for two baths.

'The thing is to put on our best clothes and walk proudly three times around the deck,' he said.

'Yes.' After a moment she added abstractedly: 'I like that young man. He was awfully nice to me last night when you'd disappeared.'

The bath steward appeared with the information that bathing was too dangerous today. They were in the midst of the wildest hurricane on the North Atlantic in ten years; there were two broken arms this morning from attempts to take baths. An elderly lady had been thrown down a staircase and was not expected to live. Furthermore, they had received the SOS[38] signal from several boats this morning.

'Will we go to help them?'

'They're all behind us, sir, so we have to leave them to the *Mauretania*. If we tried to turn in this sea the portholes would be smashed.'

This array of calamities minimized their own troubles. Having eaten a sort of luncheon and drunk the beer provided by Butterworth, they dressed and went on deck.

Despite the fact that it was only possible to progress step by step, holding on to rope or rail, more people were abroad than on the day before. Fear had driven them from their cabins, where the trunks bumped and the waves pounded the portholes, and they awaited momentarily the call to the boats. Indeed, as Adrian and Eva stood on the transverse deck above the second class, there was a bugle call, followed by a gathering of stewards and stewardesses on the deck below. But the boat was sound: it had outlasted one of its cargo – Steward James Carton was being buried at sea.

It was very British and sad. There were the rows of stiff, disciplined men and women standing in the driving rain, and there was a shape covered by the flag of the Empire that lived by the sea[39]. The chief purser read the service, a hymn was sung, the body slid off into the hurricane. With Eva's burst of wild weeping for this humble end, some last string snapped within her. Now she really didn't care. She responded eagerly when Butterworth suggested that he get some champagne to their cabin. Her mood worried Adrian; she wasn't used to so much drinking and he wondered what he ought to do. At his suggestion that they sleep instead, she merely laughed, and the bromide the doctor had sent stood untouched on the washstand. Pretending to listen to the insipidities[40] of several Mr Stacombs, he watched her; to his surprise and discomfort she seemed on intimate and even sentimental terms with Butterworth and he wondered if this was a form of revenge for his attention to Betsy D'Amido.

The cabin was full of smoke, the voices went on incessantly, the suspension of activity, the waiting for the storm's end, was getting on his nerves. They had been at sea only four days; it was like a year.

The two Mr Stacombs left finally, but Butterworth remained. Eva was urging him to go for another bottle of champagne.

'We've had enough,' objected Adrian. 'We ought to go to bed.'

'I won't go to bed!' she burst out. 'You must be crazy! You play around all you want, and then, when I find somebody I – I like, you want to put me to bed.'

'You're hysterical.'

'On the contrary, I've never been so sane.'

'I think you'd better leave us, Butterworth,' Adrian said. 'Eva doesn't know what she's saying.'

'He won't go, I won't let him go.' She clasped Butterworth's hand passionately. 'He's the only person that's been half decent to me.'

'You'd better go, Butterworth,' repeated Adrian.

The young man looked at him uncertainly.

'It seems to me you're being unjust to your wife,' he ventured.

'My wife isn't herself.'

'That's no reason for bullying her.'

Adrian lost his temper. 'You get out of here!' he cried.

The two men looked at each other for a moment in silence. Then Butterworth turned to Eva, said, 'I'll be back later,' and left the cabin.

'Eva, you've got to pull yourself together,' said Adrian when the door closed.

She didn't answer, looked at him from sullen, half-closed eyes.

'I'll order dinner here for us both and then we'll try to get some sleep.'

'I want to go up and send a wireless[41].'

'Who to?'

'Some Paris lawyer. I want a divorce.'

In spite of his annoyance, he laughed. 'Don't be silly.'

'Then I want to see the children.'

'Well, go and see them. I'll order dinner.'

He waited for her in the cabin twenty minutes. Then impatiently he opened the door across the corridor; the nurse told him that Mrs Smith had not been there.

With a sudden prescience[42] of disaster he ran upstairs, glanced in the bar, the salons, even knocked at Butterworth's door. Then a quick round of the decks, feeling his way through the black spray and rain. A sailor stopped him at a network of ropes.

'Orders are no one goes by, sir. A wave has gone over the wireless room.'

'Have you seen a lady?'

'There was a young lady here –' He stopped and glanced around. 'Hello, she's gone.'

'She went up the stairs!' Adrian said anxiously. 'Up to the wireless room!'

The sailor ran up to the boat deck; stumbling and slipping, Adrian followed. As he cleared the protected sides of the companionway[43], a tremendous body struck the boat a staggering blow and, as she keeled over to an angle of forty-five degrees, he was thrown in a helpless roll down the drenched deck, to bring up dizzy and bruised against a stanchion.

'Eva!' he called. His voice was soundless in the black storm. Against the faint light of the wireless-room window he saw the sailor making his way forward.

'Eva!'

The wind blew him like a sail up against a lifeboat. Then there was another shuddering crash, and high over his head, over the very boat, he saw a gigantic, glittering white wave, and in the split second that it balanced there he became conscious of Eva, standing beside a ventilator[44] twenty feet away. Pushing out from the stanchion, he lunged desperately toward her, just as the wave broke with a smashing

38 Save Our Souls, a radio signal used for calling for help, especially by a ship or a plane

39 the British Empire

40 *formal:* boring or dull things that a person says

41 *old-fashioned:* a radio message

42 *formal:* the condition of knowing or behaving as if you know what will happen in the future

43 a stair or ladder within the hull of a vessel; the space occupied by this stair or ladder

44 a machine that brings fresh air into a room or building and moves it around

roar. For a moment the rushing water w… …p, sweeping with enormous force towards the side, a… …an body was washed against him, and frantically he … …was swept with it back towards the rail. He felt hi… …ıst it, but desperately he held on to his burden; th… …ked slowly back, the two of them, still joined by his… …olled out exhausted on the wet planks. For a mom… …ore.

IV

Two days later, as the boat train moved … …ard Paris, Adrian tried to persuade his childre… …window at the Norman[45] countryside.

'It's beautiful,' he assured them. 'All the little fa… …ns like toys. Why, in heaven's name, won't you look?'

'I like the boat better,' said Estelle.

Her parents exchanged an infanticidal[46] glance.

'The boat is still rocking for me,' Eva said with a sl… 'Is it for you?'

'No. Somehow, it all seems a long way off. Even … …ssengers looked unfamiliar going through the customs.'

'Most of them hadn't appeared above ground[47] …'

He hesitated. 'By the way, I cashed Butterworth… …r him.'

'You're a fool. You'll never see the money ag…'

'He must have needed it pretty badly or … …me to me.'

A pale and wan girl, passing along the co… …recognized them and put her head through the doorway.

'How do you feel?'

'Awful.'

'Me, too,' agreed Miss D'Amido. 'I'm vainly hoping my fiancé will recognize me at the Gare du Nord[48]. Do you know two waves went over the wireless room?'

'So we heard,' Adrian answered dryly.

She passed gracefully along the corridor and out of their life.

'The real truth is that none of it happened,' said Adrian after a moment. 'It was a nightmare – an incredibly awful nightmare.'

'Then, where are my pearls?'

'Darling, there are better pearls in Paris. I'll take the responsibility for those pearls. My real belief is that you saved the boat.'

'Adrian, let's never get to know anyone else, but just stay together always – just we two.'

He tucked her arm under his and they sat close. 'Who do you suppose those Adrian Smiths on the boat were?' he demanded. 'It certainly wasn't me.'

'Nor me.'

'It was two other people,' he said, nodding to himself. 'There are so many Smiths in this world.'

45 adjective used to describe things in and from Normandy, a region in the north of France

46 adjective for *infanticide*, the crime of killing a baby or very young child. Used comically here

47 on the deck of the ship, rather than in the cabins on the lower decks

48 a train station in Paris